Pagan Homeschooling

A Guide to Adding Spirituality to Your Child's Education

by
Kristin Madden

Spilled Candy Books
Niceville, Florida USA

Pagan Homeschooling
Copyright 2002

By Kristin Madden

Published by: Spilled Candy Books,
Spilled Candy Publications
Post Office Box 5202
Niceville, FL 32578-5202
Staff@spilledcandy.com
http://www.spilledcandy.com

ISBN: 1-892718-421 (trade paperback)

Library of Congress Card Number: 2002112155
First edition

Cover Art copyright 2002 by Jillian Pate

Dedication

For Karl,
You inspire and motivate me every moment of every day.

About the Author

Kristin Madden is the author of four Llewellyn books, including the bestselling *Pagan Parenting*. She was raised in a shamanic home and has explored both Eastern and Western mystic paths and New Age methods since 1972. She is a Druid, tutor, and tutor mentor for the Order of Bards, Ovates, and Druids and a practicing astrologer. She is on the governing Boards of Silver Moon Health Services and The Ardantane Project, both non-profit organizations incorporated in New Mexico. Kristin is also the Director of the Ardantane School of Shamanic Arts.

As a homeschooling mother, Kristin is active in local and global homeschooling communities, both pagan and secular. She organizes play groups and field trips locally as well as children's rituals for each of the eight neopagan festivals.

Kristin has been a workshop leader and a speaker at pagan conferences and metaphysical centers across the United States since 1994. She has been a guest on radio shows throughout the United States and Canada. Her work and interviews with her have appeared in a wide variety of magazines and newsletters throughout North America and Europe.

Other works by author

Shamanic Guide to Death and Dying
(Llewellyn 1999)

Pagan Parenting
(Llewellyn 2000)

Mabon: Celebrating the Autumn Equinox
(Llewellyn 2002)

The Book of Shamanic Healing
(Llewellyn 2002).

Table of Contents

Pagan Homeschooling

Chapter One
Why Homeschool?

Imagine for a moment that you have the opportunity to see every milestone of your children's young lives. You are there for first steps and first words. You are there when they learn to spell their own names. You guide them through their first addition problems. You get to see the light in their eyes when they grasp their first scientific concepts. You read the first story they write and critique their first essays.

Imagine that learning happens in your family all the time. It is a free-flowing life process through which everyone benefits. Many of us say that everything in life is a learning opportunity. Visualize a life that allows you and your children to live that belief fully. Learning is no longer limited to a concentrated and rigid schedule each week. Your children are able to progress at their own speeds, making the best of each one's unique learning style. That awful Monday morning feeling no longer exists, and there is no "hump" day. Each and every day you have the freedom to choose your experience and to share it with your children.

Imagine not having to abandon your children to a compulsory school system where both teacher competence and enthusiasm vary greatly. Allow yourself to consider the possibility of a life in which you and your children can socialize and learn in a healthy, supportive atmosphere of like-minded people. Your children can ask as many questions as they want whenever they want. If they are having a bad day or need a break, they can do so freely. They are encouraged to follow learning tangents sparked by other topics. Picture your children growing up in an environment that does not include gangs, school violence, sexual harassment, religious discrimination, or the "in-crowd."

This is the real-life experience of a great many home educators around the world. These are families who have chosen to take charge of their lives and reject compulsory public educational systems. They are creating their lives in ways that allow them to find a better way for themselves and their children. As a result, they are contributing to a better educated and more balanced future society.

The reasons for home educating are as varied as the families who choose this option. Each parent, even within one family, usually has unique beliefs, thoughts, and processes that went into making this decision. One might assume that pagan homeschoolers choose this option for religious reasons, but the truth is that this is neither the most common nor the most important factor for the majority. Most of us make this choice for the same reason any other parent would. We do not do this in order to avoid life, but to enable our children to live a happy and fulfilling life now and learn to create the life they want as adults.

An article written about me in 2001 reported that I was considering homeschooling so as not to compromise our family's strong beliefs. While overall this was a good article, it was not really accurate in a couple of respects. Not only was I actively homeschooling at the time of that interview and had been for quite some time, but religious beliefs were not my main reason for home educating our son. In fact, when our son attended a mainstream daycare center, we did not compromise or hide our beliefs.

Like most parents, we want what is best for our child in all areas of life. We have made the best choices for our particular family with regard to educational excellence, safety, and spirituality. Certainly the ability to include spirituality and prevent fear-based reactions from schoolmates is an added benefit to home education, but we do not limit our interactions to pagans. In fact, our homeschool group consists of pagans, Christians, and others that have less defined labels for their spirituality or are not spiritual at all. We all get along just fine and are teaching our children about tolerance in the process.

However, some parents do begin to investigate home education for a variety of religious reasons. In my case, I wanted our son to have a more expansive and spiritual educational experience than was found in compulsory schools. I was also getting very tired of the constant need to educate the staff at his pre-school center. Even though he was only there part-time, I was continually surprised at the preponderance of Christian materials and the total lack of discussion on any other religion. For example, no mention of Hanukkah or Kwanzaa was ever made. Furthermore, I wanted Karl to learn academically with a conscious awareness of the interconnections of all things.

The director of this center was always professional about our discussions and did stop giving out blatantly Christian materials. She also stopped the viewing of Christian videos in our son's class (and only in that class). But it was a discussion that should not have taken place more than once or twice. There was an obvious assumption among the staff that all families were Christian. In truth and unknown to the center, there was one other pagan family and one Buddhist family with children enrolled there at the time.

Several parents I have spoken with report that this type of unconscious yet pervasive religious influence in public schools was a motivating factor in their search for alternative educational choices. A couple of parents refused to allow their children to participate in overtly Christian activities. While the schools worked around this most of the time, it created a separation between pagan children and their classmates.

For many of us, the investigation into home education was not motivated by a desire to pretend that other religions don't exist or to completely isolate our children from differing beliefs. Most of us do not feel that public schools have the authority or the right to introduce religion in any form with the exception of an overview during specific cultural studies. We object to an assumption that all children are of one or two religions or that it is acceptable to focus solely on any religion.

This assumption leads to an implication that mainstream monotheistic religions are the best or the most acceptable. Schools in all fifty of the United States have allowed the use of school property for religious meetings. Some of these are legal student-led religious groups that meet after school is over. Others are fairly slick campaigns run by adults with the sole focus of getting children to convert. Surveys of children attending these schools often report a belief that the school endorses the events. This belief is reinforced when they see their teachers or other school staff attending these religious meetings – on public school property.

This type of action frequently creates an attitude that places one religion above others, making children of different spiritual backgrounds feel left out, uncomfortable, or even afraid. This is not the role of public schools. In the United States, we have a Constitutional right to separation of Church and State. Unless you enroll your children in a religious school, the choice of when and how to introduce spirituality and religion should be left to the parents or legal guardians alone.

In the spring of 2001, I sent out a questionnaire to families that have previously, are currently, or are considering home educating their children. This went out on several email lists and by post or hand-delivery to parents that follow a pagan or alternative religious spiritual path. I also gleaned a fair amount of information through discussions with other parents online and in person.

By far, the majority of parents that responded to my questionnaire made their choice based on academic reasons, often after experiencing problems with public school systems. It would seem that a growing number of families are dissatisfied with public education and are not willing to simply sit by and hope for change, nor are they willing to allow their children to suffer while they are working to change the system.

Several parents brought their children home when school officials refused to allow testing for a potential jump to a new grade. These children were routinely performing well above their grade levels. Some were so bored that they began to act out in class. Parents report that behavioral issues have either disappeared or have been significantly reduced and their children continue to succeed in work at least one grade level above where their age would place them in a public school system.

In a few cases, the schools labeled children as learning disabled or hyperactive. Parents were concerned that such labels would follow children throughout their school careers and influence their lives in many ways. One mother was advised by a teacher to put her kindergartner on medication for ADD. When her pediatrician told her that her son was a normal boy for his age and was not in need of any medication, the teacher singled him out for abuse, even telling him in front of the class that he deserved to be called a loser. Needless to say, that was his very last day in public school.

Problems with public school systems were a factor in my decision to explore home education. We experienced issues with violence in the classroom for the first time when Karl was just two years old. This was not an isolated incident and the problems continued on and off until I pulled him out at four years old. There was even one situation where a teacher sat by and watched three older children surround our son and push him down. Fortunately, I had just arrived to pick him up. In spite of the fact that I had seen everything, the school refused to discipline the teacher and I received no apology from anyone. That was the last straw. This was at one of the "best" preschools in our area. Most parents were not around during the odd hours to see these things. I made it a point to drop in unexpectedly at various times throughout the day.

For decades, parents have cited safety as one of their reasons for home education. With the increase in school shootings and other violence in and around school communities, home education is on the rise. Many parents are deciding that they are not willing to take the chance. Even children who have not been physically injured in school violence may bear emotional scars that can take a lifetime to overcome. Children should not be afraid to go to school. That is not conducive to learning nor does it contribute to the holistic well being of our children.

Most spiritual or religious parents tend to consider the spiritual aspects of their children's lives as being extremely important. Pagan home educators often incorporate religious elements into their teaching or use aspects of their spirituality, such as the Wheel of the Year and lunar phases, as teaching tools. I will explore this further in later chapters.

But more than that, we consider the benefits of home education on our children, emotionally, mentally, academically, energetically, and spiritually. We see our children as complete individuals for whom we have accepted a tremendous responsibility. We need to be aware of the impact of environment on their interconnected levels of being.

The human energy field continues to develop through adolescence, right along with our physical bodies, emotions, and mental abilities. Each typical stage of child development is accompanied by a corresponding stage in energetic development. Most school systems are not qualified to recognize, let alone understand or properly handle this. Therefore, it is up to parents to determine what environments are appropriate for our children, and this is likely to vary with each individual child. I deal with this in detail in the next chapter.

With homeschooled children winning national spelling bees, scoring in the highest percentiles on college entrance exams, and being actively recruited by Ivy League schools, academics are a good reason to choose home education. This option enables parents to recognize that each child learns in a unique way. It allows parents to best support their children's individual learning styles. It is important to understand that academics will not suffer simply because the adults in a family do not have advanced degrees in every subject.

Homeschooling parents are not fooled into believing we cannot teach our children at least as well as a teacher who has a full classroom and answers to both administration and parents for relatively low pay. Teachers today are limited by school budgets that affect salaries, supplies, class sizes, and field trips. Because of the low pay, stress, and potential for violence in the schools, there is a shortage of qualified and enthusiastic teachers in many areas.

Charter schools have offered many of us a fine

alternative to public schooling. In some areas, these students are exceeding all expectations. Students consistently outperform peers on standardized tests, they have access to a variety of programs beyond academics, and parents feel their children are safe in these places.

However, this is not always the case. Some charter schools have extremely low test scores and children do not seem to get the attention they need to learn basic skills. Furthermore, the competition for funding has led to a focus on marketing that can include student advertising. When the funds are not there, programs and supplies disappear.

As parents, we have been teaching our children since the day they were born. Many of us have at least as much education as public school teachers. We do not ignore the fact that smaller classroom sizes and individual support are what school systems attempt to create in order to raise grades and esteem and reduce classroom problems. An atmosphere of loving support, individual attention, and a feeling of safety only encourage children to grow up self-assured and eager to learn.

The parents I spoke with cited these as their top reasons for home educating:

- problems with public school teachers or administrations
- large classroom sizes and fewer good teachers
- the irrational competition that can arise in schools
- lowering of school standards/desire for children to have the tools they need to succeed
- the idea that only nerds or geeks (or worse) do well in school

- school violence and harassment
- inappropriate religious experiences

Parents do not want their children in this type of energy nor do they want to take the chance that their children will be the ones falling through the cracks while teachers focus on the average majority.

Some parents in my survey have children with special needs. Rather than accept a belief that they could not possibly handle the needs of their own children, these parents took a leap of faith and brought their children home. All of the children whose stories I heard had significant improvements in behavior, learning ability, self-esteem, and happiness as a result.

Special needs children do require additional education, creativity, flexibility, and patience on the part of parents, whether they are homeschooled or not. I know parents who have used their innate creativity and trusted their own inspiration in finding unique ways to assist their children in learning. Some of these children have gone far beyond what teachers and doctors ever believed they could.

One child did most of his schoolwork upside down for almost a year. Another needed to learn in very small time increments. Another learned best while going up and down steps and yet another needed an extremely structured setting due highly functional autism. In a school setting these unusual methods would not be allowed. But the parents in these situations were aware and flexible enough to work with their children rather than attempting to force a more "normal" method. Each situation has been a success.

Not all parents home educate as the result of bad experiences with or bad feelings regarding public schools or daycare centers. One of the parents who responded to my questionnaire was homeschooled herself, along with several people in her family. She reports that everyone in her family who was homeschooled fluently speaks at least three languages and has had valuable training in several arts and trades. With such wonderful successes, this was what she wanted her children to experience. This is a good example of how beneficial home education can be.

Other parents in my survey chose to home educate because it was the natural thing to do. It felt right to them and flowed easily from all they had been doing since their children were born. They stated that this is a lifestyle choice more than anything else. Teachable moments are everywhere and these families do not want to miss out on sharing in the growth of their families by sending their children away five days each week.

All of the homeschooling families I have spoken with cherish the special bond that develops through home education. Certainly there are difficult times when the children want to scream and the parents think how easy it would be to have their children just go away for a few hours a day. That happens in any relationship from time to time. But we learn a great deal about our children and ourselves as we work through the tough times and build those special bonds as a family.

For the most part, home educating parents deeply appreciate the fact that we learn right along with our children. We feel blessed to be able to share in their growth on so many levels. In the process, we gain some unique insight into the members of our family, while getting to know each other on a deep and holistic level.

The psychic bonds we develop through pregnancy and infancy are strengthened as our children grow up. Many of us are able to remain in tune with each other through these psychic connections. Certainly our children develop into independent and self-sufficient individuals, but that unique connection to parents remains. The innate knowledge that something is wrong or that a child needs to contact us does not fade as it does with many families. Because we share a common environment and common focus rather being separate physically and mentally for many hours each day, the energetic attunement between parent and child continues to resonate harmoniously.

Most homeschoolers love the freedom that home education brings to our lives. Our days are not set by a governing authority that knows nothing about our lifestyle or our children's needs and strengths. We can provide an extremely small class or enroll them in a larger public class, depending on their needs at any given time. We can sit and do worksheets in the morning and go to the zoo in the afternoon if we like. If an interest arises, we can spend three whole days studying the Space Shuttle.

We learn all day every day and all year long. There is no pressure to complete a certain set of studies or pass specific tests by the end of a school year in order to advance. The lack of an imposed schedule allows us to explore our children's learning styles in subtle ways, giving top priority to emotional security and the healthy development of self-esteem.

Specialists in child development consider developing a solid base in social and emotional security to be more important early on than all the new tools and toys intended to stimulate our children's minds. We need to focus on the heart before the head and guide both into balance as our children grow older. The development of security, trust, respect, and love between parents and children is a necessary foundation for holistically healthy kids.

Many child development experts, perhaps most notably education pioneer John Holt, have written that children are born with a natural curiosity and an innate ability to learn. We do not need to make them do anything, they learn no matter what we do. The brain of a baby is constantly changing, laying out and strengthening neural pathways each day. All it needs is appropriate stimulation that builds emotional security. As a result, adults hold a significant responsibility to ensure children learn positively and are exposed to supportive, beneficial experiences.

If you are considering home education, take a moment to consider the checklist below. If you believe it is best for your family but don't think you can do it, please reconsider. You would be extremely surprised to know the wide variety of people who have taken the leap and never looked back, including those who have given up one income, found creative ways to bring in additional money, or have managed to maintain their jobs and homeschool at the same time. If you believe in it, you can make it happen.

Is Home Education Right For You?

- Do you want to be a larger part of your children's learning experiences?
- Do you want more involvement in your children's lives?
- Are you completely happy with the education your children receive in school? Are they encouraged by teachers and fellow students to explore fully all aspects of a topic of interest?
- Do you object to the stress and unreasonable workload your children appear to have?
- Are you completely happy with the treatment your children receive from teachers, administrators, and classmates?
- Do your children thrive in school? Are you happy with the behaviors and beliefs they pick up in school?
- Do you worry about violence, peer pressure, or sexual harassment at school?
- Do you or your children ever feel the need to hide your spirituality around any member of the school community?
- Do you wish your children could incorporate more spirituality, tolerance, and respect All Life into their academics?
- Do you believe that learning should be encouraged throughout all of life rather than abruptly stopping at the end of school day, week, and semester?

By now, it should be obvious that the reasons for choosing home education are as unique as each individual. There are a great number of similarities but ultimately, the choice is a highly personal one that involves a wide range of factors relating to the family as a whole. This is not a choice that should be made lightly, and it is not the right decision for all families.

But for those of you who found a feeling of joy, hope, and satisfaction in the initial paragraphs of this chapter, this may be just the right route for your family. If this appeals to you, do not simply take my word for it. Explore the resources listed throughout this book. Speak with people who are homeschooling and find out the pros and cons for them. If possible, speak with adults who were homeschooled and children who are currently being homeschooled to get their opinions as well.

As pagan parents, we are certainly concerned with our children's potential academic and social success. More than that, we are aware that our children's hearts and spirits are at stake. With an understanding of energy systems, the guidance of our Gods, and the availability of a wide range of home education resources, an increasing number of us are realizing that we can provide the best all-around education for our children at home. This is the choice we have made to preserve the innate wholeness and spark for life our children bring into this world…and perhaps we regain some of that for ourselves in the process.

Recommended Reading

Albert, David H. (1999) *And the Skylark Sings with Me - Adventures in Homeschooling and Community-Based Education.* New Society Pub.

Cohen, Cafi (2000) *Homeschooler's College Admissions Handbook.* Prima Publishing.

Dobson, Linda (2000) *Homeschoolers' Success Stories: 15 Adults and 12 Young People Share the Impact That Homeschooling Has Made on Their Lives.* Prima Publishing.

Gatto, John Taylor (2000) *A Different Kind of Teacher: Solving the Crisis of American Schooling.* Berkeley Hills Books.

Guterson, David (1993) *Family Matters: Why Homeschooling Makes Sense.* Harvest Books.

Holt, John (1990) *Learning All the Time.* Perseus Pr.

Holt, John (1995) *How Children Fail.* Perseus Pr.

Holt, John (1995) *How Children Learn.* Perseus Pr.

Layne, Marty (2000) *Learning At Home: A Mother's Guide To Homeschooling.* Sea Change Publications.

Resources

National Home Education Network
NHEN
P.O. Box 41067
Long Beach, CA 90853
FAX: (413) 581-1463
http://www.nhen.org/toc/toc-index.html

A to Z Home's Cool
Homeschooling Website
http://www.gomilpitas.com/homeschooling/

Chapter Two
Energetic Considerations

As pagan parents, we are aware that our children are much more than their brains and physical bodies. As a result, it is our responsibility to guide and safeguard them on many levels. When we talk about energetic considerations in raising and educating children, we are referring to a wide range of aspects of being. This will include the development and maintenance of energy systems, astrological influences, meditation and breathing techniques, healing methods, and even the food we eat.

The first three of these aspects are most important to the home educator, and those will be covered in some detail in this chapter. However, most of these will be discussed at some point in this book, whether in relation to developing curricula and unit studies, or integrating spirituality into education. I write from my personal experience and what I have learned by speaking with countless other homeschooling parents. Your experience may vary and I encourage you to explore and experiment in each of these areas within your own family. Take our experiences and use them as a starting point for discovering what is best for you and your family.

Development of Energy Systems

An understanding of the development of the human energy system can be extremely beneficial, not only when working on a metaphysical level but also during everyday activities. Our energy systems influence and are influenced by everything in our environment: mental, physical, emotional, and spiritual. This plays an important role both in the decision to homeschool and in the methods we use in the process.

From the moment they are born, our children remain connected to parents energetically. An energetic umbilical cord replaces the physical one. Just as the mother physically feeds her child *in utero* through the umbilical cord, so does she continue to feed her child energetically after birth. This is normally also true of the father, with whom a similar cord develops.

A significant amount of a parent's personal energy flows to their children through these cords. In this way, we buffer our children against potentially damaging influences, we support their development on many levels, and we are able to receive psychic information from them. This is one of the ways in which we know if a child is hurt or upset or if something just isn't right.

The infant's energy system begins to separate from that of the mother by the time the toddler stage is reached. This is paralleled by a more complete integration into the physical body. This is accompanied by the ability to recognize and respond to one's own name. During this time, children begin to learn the language and customs of their family. Thought processes become more refined and children experiment as they learn how this world works.

At this point, learning has already begun as a natural progression of integration in this reality. The child needs no encouragement to learn, although this certainly supports and can strengthen the process. As parents, we teach in many ways but largely through example as our children learn through our words and actions.

This is a vulnerable time in the development of our children's energy systems. They have no psychic buffers and their chakras are more open than those of adults. Protection against destructive environments and intense magick are vital at these young ages. Young children need their parents emotionally and energetically on all levels of being.

We are their buffers and their protection. We decide what they will be exposed to and what we will protect them from, in most cases. While energy systems develop along with physical, emotional, and mental abilities, children are wide open to external influences. They pick up on issues within the family and they are susceptible to the energy of any area that they may spend time in. The choice of babysitters and daycare takes on a whole new aspect when we consider energetic protection.

Conflict, violence, and uncontrolled emotions have the potential to damage children's energy systems. Children who have been raised in environments lacking in safety, support, and unconditional love act out as older children and adults. The result is juvenile crime, teen pregnancy, and suicide. These are not bad kids. They are wounded kids who are unable to feel a connection to Nature, other people, or their inner selves-- and they are crying out for help.

Children instinctively know to go to a trusted person for comfort and protection when they feel unsafe or uncomfortable. They may hide behind us or climb into our laps. They understand on a very deep level that the energy field of a trusted adult will support and protect them from potentially damaging influences. We provide the buffers they need until their own defenses develop. Without that buffering, there is nothing to prevent the wounding, even in what we might consider minor situations such as teasing by peers.

I have met children who were raised in violent and non-nurturing environments. These children had no adult protection in difficult situations from very young ages. By the time their personal defenses developed, several of these children no longer needed them. They learned to shut down completely all, but those chakras essential for physical survival.

Many of these children overcame their challenges and went on to become successful adults. But many of them retain energetic wounds and find it difficult to trust others. Some also still hold a very tough outer shell with impenetrable defenses that go up at the slightest indication of a threat. This is not a chance we want to take with our own children, especially with the prevalence of school violence. This one of the reasons why many families home educate.

Our children face a continual barrage of violence,

sex, social judgment, and more each day. One need only turn on the television, walk down a city street, or peruse available movies and electronic games to see this in full force. The shows that are directed toward children, along with the accompanying marketing push, astonish and sadden me. Producers and writers are obviously not going to make changes, so it is up to the parents and legal guardians to decide what is appropriate.

Most of us agree that our children's emotional and spiritual welfare is not worth the risk of allowing marketers and media to baby-sit our children. We want more control over what they are exposed to. We do not want to isolate them completely from this reality, but exposing our children to make-believe violence and disrespect is no more acceptable than it would be to expose them to the real thing.

This is what most public school children have been raised with. It may begin as early as infancy when parents don't realize how open and aware children are. This is what is cool and trendy. Children are expected to know about the popular television shows and wear the right clothes in school. Sadly, it also has a tremendous influence on behaviors and attitudes. This is not the type of socialization that homeschoolers want for our children.

As our children grow up, the need for the energetic supplement provided by the energy umbilical cord diminishes. As a result, the energy cord shrinks, though it usually doesn't completely disappear until after the death of both individuals. Eventually around the age of seven, chakra filters begin to form, providing a degree of protection for these young energy systems.

This is not an automatic and complete protection. The development of these filters takes some time, and their ability to defend our children is dependent on many factors. Some children have a greater ability to ground out[1] damaging and intense energy provided it is not a constant barrage. Other children are naturally more sensitive and need to learn this basic protection.

Even children with a natural ability to shield and ground energy can react with nightmares, insecurities, hostility, and other behavioral problems as the result of shocked and damaged chakras when confronted with an influx of extreme energy. They may also exhibit physical problems in the area where the damage to the energy field has occurred. This influx may come from other adults, media, or other children

Schools are full of subtle yet persistent energy drains and potential shocks to the young energy system. The lack of security and energetic awareness is not conducive to learning or healthy development. For many children, it is most definitely destructive, particularly if they do not fit in or are more sensitive than other children.

Many children will form a type of etheric cord, bonding them to teachers. In some cases, this can be a very beneficial situation. It can provide an energetic buffer and a feeling of security. This can help a child gain some healthy independence from parents when daycare or public school is the only option.

However, this can be detrimental in certain situations. Children in institutions with a great deal of staff turnover can develop abandonment and trust issues. This can even occur among toddlers when a favorite teacher is out sick, leaves, or is seen working with children in another room. It can certainly be dangerous when the energy a child receives from a teacher is uncontrolled or full of negativity, no matter how the teacher behaves in class.

There are some children who cannot form these bonds to teachers. They become lost and hurt when separated from parents. Some people might say that children need to toughen up to survive in this world. My opinion, and that of most homeschoolers I know, is that these are children and should be cared for as such.

Children have every right to be understood and respected for their individuality. This is as much a part of our duty as parents and educators as is offering guidance and protection. It is vital that we accept the full responsibility involved in the choice to bring children into this world. This includes doing whatever is necessary to support the healthy development of body, mind, and spirit. There is plenty of time as adults to be tough. We are not raising soldiers--we are raising spiritual beings in human form who deserve every opportunity to grow into healthy, balanced adults.

It is true that some children tend to be more emotionally and psychically sensitive than others. These children often benefit greatly from home education for many reasons. These are children who will soak up external influences and the emotions of those around them without even realizing these feelings belong to someone else. They may find themselves becoming caught up in the energies present and can feel lost or uncomfortable even with a parent present.

Sensitive children can find the necessary buffers

they need at home. This is particularly true when their parents have some understanding of energetic influences and the chakra system. In pagan homes, these children are guided and encouraged to develop protective measures and to learn to differentiate their feelings from those of others. They are taught to ground extraneous and potentially damaging energy out of their systems and to replenish themselves from healthy sources, such as the Earth, the Sky, spirit guides, etc.

This is often a part of the homeschooling lifestyle among pagan families. We acknowledge that our children's energetic development is equally as important as their academic and extracurricular development. Supporting this is part of our lifestyle. Teaching the methods necessary to maintain a healthy energy system is seen as integral to homeschool work because we recognize that all facets of our education are interrelated.

Pagan parents often strive to develop their own psychic abilities. They do this for their own personal development as well as to be able to teach and guide their children in using their own innate abilities. Parents also do this because it strengthens their natural intuition regarding their children. The use of these abilities can warn families of potential conflicts or discomfort in children. It can let a parent know when a child is hurt or in danger. It can also become a cheap and easy means of communication between parent and child.

My mother and I often joke about not needing the telephone. Sometimes this psychic communication comes through in words, and sometimes it is just a feeling. Now that I am a mother myself, I find myself sharing these same experiences with my son. And the more parents I speak with, the more common I find this experience to be. Below I have outlined three exercises to encourage your own ability to be in contact with your children at a much deeper level. Each exercise becomes more powerful with practice and is appropriate for children as young as four years old.

Exercise: Shake Hands[2]

This is one of the simplest and most profound ways to learn to feel the human energy field. It may help to rub your hands together before and after. If you wish, you may count down from ten to one beforehand.

Sit or stand together. Hold out your hands as though you were going to shake hands. Stop just before actually touching the other person's hand. Notice any feeling or impression you get when your hands are very close together. Many people will feel a warmth, tingling, or resistance similar to touching two North (or two South) poles of a magnet together.

Now, play with this by slowly moving your hands further apart and then closer together. Be aware of any feelings or impressions that either person receives. Learn to trust your instincts. Practice this at different times to get a feel for how the aura changes. It will normally feel different after work or school than it might be after meditation or ritual.

Exercise to Develop Psychic Awareness

We all have heard people say that they just don't like the "vibes" at a certain place. Perhaps you have been to a place that just didn't feel right. Maybe you have known instantly upon entering a room that the previous occupants have been fighting. This is basic psychic awareness: the ability to understand the energies you come in contact with.

This can be an important ability for both parents and children to develop. Not only does it teach us to differentiate personal feelings from those around us, but it also encourages us all to trust our impressions about people, things, and places. It provides us with a way to validate these feelings and to know when psychic protection is really necessary.

Begin in your bedroom or in the center of your house. Count down from one to ten. Taking three deep, diaphragmatic breaths, blow all tensions, worries, and thoughts into a pink bubble. Release the bubble to the universe to handle for the time being. Then go through your house, spending about ten minutes in each room.

Enter each room with eyes closed. Notice how you feel simply by walking in. Now open your eyes and look around. Notice what attracts and what repels your attention. Gaze upon each of these things, releasing personal judgments. Does the feeling remain once your critique is gone? Be aware of how this space makes you feel.

Practice this same exercise, with eyes open, around your neighborhood, at stores, and at work. If there is an argument, an emotional outburst, or a time of lovemaking in your home, take note of how that room feels to you the next day. With practice, you will move beyond your own personal judgments into a truly intuitive experience of the energies of each place. At that point, you can accurately gauge how healthy or clear any space is and what may be going on with its occupants.

As toddlers, children reach the "Mine" phase where ownership is assigned to the people, places, and things in their lives. It may also be assigned to attractive items that belong to others. This phase is often accompanied by the beginning of imaginative play. By this age, toddlers are fairly well integrated into their bodies, and they generally understand that they are individual beings, separate from their parents.

These "terrible" twos and threes are a unique and often difficult time for the child. The perception of oneself as an individual occurs on all levels. As children test their boundaries and want to be more independent, many are not sure they are ready to be a separate being yet. They alternate between developing a defined personal auric field and being psychically connected to other life forms, as they were as infants.

Unless your child has a real desire for focused education at this age, you might consider waiting to begin something formal. No matter what educational style you choose when they are older, this is the age to unschool[3]. While it is true that our children are like mental sponges at early ages and many people suggest starting formal schooling young, they are "sponges" on all levels of being and this needs to be handled with care.

The toddler years are when the individuality is developing. This is when children are learning the ways of their families and cultures. Even though most of adults have limited conscious memories of this time in our lives, the things we experience and learn during this period stay with us throughout our lives.

Consider what you want your children to carry with them through life. Do you want them to perceive this life and our culture as a rigid testing ground where we need to work hard simply to stay ahead? Should their focus be always on a definite goal and on what can be attained or bought when they reach that goal? Some people may say this is how modern society is and our children need to be prepared for it. These families want their children to have a good life and be able to afford to live well. This is true, but all families want that.

Chances are good that families with this type of focus would not choose homeschooling except as a last resort. Homeschooling families do want their children to succeed and to live happily. However, producing future CEOs and vice presidents is not usually a goal of home education. The goal is to support our children in achieving what they want to achieve and encouraging their natural abilities to become happy, healthy, and balanced adults. If they choose to go on and become CEOs that's wonderful, provided it is what they want for themselves.

During early childhood, homeschooling families recognize that learning is occurring in a great many areas. As a result, we go with what flows best for our children and our individual families. Because the young child is psychically so open, this is an ideal age to begin to introduce the basic concepts of your spiritual path. Children at these ages have an innate spirituality that only needs some encouragement to take form.

The world is a wonder to explore for young children. It can remain this way for older children and adults if we can maintain that adventurous attitude. Little ones love stories about the Moon and nature spirits. Songs, chants, and simple rituals can be great fun at this age. This is also the time to introduce nighttime rituals, stories, altars, and stone collections.

Toddlers have limited attention spans coupled with an abundance of physical energy. For this reason, physically active rituals and exercises may be a beneficial complement to any educational method you may choose to use. Beginning yoga, dances, songs, and easy games are favorites among children at this age. Rather than institute a rigorous training in religion at this age, parents tend to focus more on the spirituality behind the religion. Toddlers respond best to an introduction to the concepts of love, tolerance, respect for All Life, and learning to connect with that divine Source or Creator.

The child's energy field begins to develop its own personal protection around age seven. The energy umbilical cord starts to diminish as filters form over the child's chakras. These filters gain strength and resiliency as we grow up. This is often the time when children exert their independence to a significant degree through extracurricular activities, playing on their own or with friends, or even having sleepovers. These energetic buffers insulate children to the point where they are more comfortable with increased amounts of time away from parents.

By this age, children have assumed many of the customs of their family and culture. Even in families who believe in life beyond this physical reality, peer pressure and the images received through mainstream society may initiate blocks to children's interdimensional awareness. The desire to make friends and fit in at school can overpower a family's beliefs. It may also create a need for the child to develop two distinct sides of Self and to keep these sides as separate as possible.

This need for dual identities is a concern for pagan home educators. A direct experience with other worlds and a personal relationship with Deities or spirit guides is a large part of our daily existence. Pagans who were not raised in metaphysical homes may have worked very hard to regain access to the spirit world and their own inner selves. They do not want their children to have to go through this as well.

For some pagan parents, this is a factor in our choice to home educate. All of us appreciate the opportunity to raise our children in a more open and psychically supportive atmosphere. Many of us take advantage of the freedom inherent in home education to encourage the development of these abilities in our children.

The elementary school ages are perfect for instituting a loose training program, provided it is fun and does not evolve into stressful work for the child. However, this emphasis on fun does not mean a lack of seriousness. In many pagan traditions, children are dedicated to the path of their parents at this age and may begin to participate in ritual workings other than holiday celebrations. In some religions, children begin a formal training system by this age. Children at these ages are ready to learn the responsibility and sanctity of a spiritual path. But if they are pushed too hard, their self-esteem may suffer and they may reject all that you want them to learn.

Parents can work with their children's developing energy systems, focusing largely on supporting the abilities they already manifest or show an interest in. Games and stories are excellent methods, particularly when they include everyone's participation, making it a family affair. This benefits all of us in the process because it encourages healthy family bonds and gives older family members a chance to review the basics.

This is an ideal time to introduce exercises that support or increase a child's ability to access memory and use intuition to gain useful information. When I was a child, this was a major focus of my training between the ages of seven and nine. I can honestly say that it helped a great deal with my confidence and ability to retrieve information when necessary.

Exercise: Answer Faeries[4]

This exercise came out of my own experience with helping spirits, what my Saami ancestors call *saivo* spirits, and it has been adapted for dreaming. The *saivo* are generally nature spirits, although they can be little people who live in the Earth. They act as helpers and go-betweens for us when we need assistance.

I chose to use faeries for two reasons. One reason is because they have become a common element in our culture. The other reason is because they are often related to Nature and they are completely non-threatening. Those of you who are well versed in the various kinds of faery folk may want to distinguish these faeries as *devas* or Nature elves, as opposed to the Great Elves or the Sidhe of Celtic paganism.

First, count down from ten to one, in your usual manner, just before going to sleep. You may either do this for your child or older children may do this for themselves. In that calm, relaxed place, have the child call on the Answer Faeries to come join them and help him answer their question.

Give the child a few moments and ask what the faeries look like. Ask how many have come to play tonight. Have the child greet them and thank them for coming to help. Even if you are not really aware of them, greet them and thank them yourself. Now, guide your child to tell them what help is needed. Help your child get as specific as possible. You may wish to discuss this in advance.

Guide your child to ask for their help tonight and bring back an answer within a specific amount of time. Some people believe that three days, or seventy-two hours, is a magickal period of time. It doesn't really matter unless you believe it does. Asking for an answer by the following morning works just as well although some very involved issues may take some time before a complete answer is received.

Mental abilities begin to develop in the elementary school ages, usually through the pre-teen years. In our society, the use of one's mental capacities is encouraged from a very young age. Parents may find that their children do not fully integrate math and reading until after the age of seven, sometimes not until eight or nine years of age.

This is not a reflection on parental teaching abilities, nor does it indicate a lack in children's abilities or intelligence. While it is true that some children find strengths in certain areas earlier than others, the fact is that this is the natural age for the development of the mental chakras. This is when analytical thought and the ability to understand these concepts naturally manifest. Attempting to force these to develop earlier can result in damaged energy systems, loss of self-esteem, and a dislike for the subject in question.

This activation of one's mental abilities is also accompanied by an increase in imagination. Children at these ages can become geniuses at make believe. They truly seem to create whatever they pretend. This aspect can be of great value to any spiritual training process. Pagan home educators often determine what educational elements to include based on where children are in their mental, emotional, spiritual, and psychic development.

During this early phase of creativity and imagination, visualization games and exercises are recommended to help the child gain self-knowledge and to develop stronger connections to helping spirits or Deities. This is a period when a more directed form of training in academics and religion is possible to many children, but it remains important to maintain an awareness of the child's energetic state and allow methods to be child-led whenever possible.

Parents have had great success introducing sitting meditation to children as young as three. However, this may be most productive during the early school years. As long as parents are mindful of the attention span of each child and allow for giggle fits every now and then, it can be a truly wonderful practice to share with your children. It can also provide them a firm basis in grounding, centering, and opening to their spirit guides and inner selves. I recommend combining passive silent meditation with a more active form of either guided meditation or shamanic journeying.

The benefits of an ability to relax and go within cannot be overemphasized. This is equally true for children with special needs, including Attention Deficit Disorder/Attention Deficit Hyperactivity Disorder and Obsessive Compulsive Disorder. When a child is able to relax the body-mind and gain control over behaviors and thoughts, even those normally considered automatic, they cease to be victims and reestablish themselves as creators of their own experience.

The Power of Breath

Meditation, yoga, shamanic journeying, and certain forms of ritual can all provide a means of relaxation. However, *pranayama*, a yogic method of controlling the breath, is one of the simplest yet most powerful methods to gain this control. *Prana* is the flow of energy through the universe, and it is often perceived as the link between body and mind.

This flow is essential to the healthy development of energy systems and the maintenance of a healthy body, mind, and spirit. When energetic flow is blocked or disrupted, the individual will experience illness or injury in a way that is associated with that disruption. Often this shows up as a physical condition near the blockage, but it can just as easily manifest through emotional, academic, or social issues. *Prana* is believed to move through the breath. Therefore, gaining control over the breath can give us access to the flow of *prana* throughout our systems.

The breath is something we all take for granted. It is automatic. Most of us never think about it, yet the cycle of inhalation and exhalation continues to repeat itself. We do have some control over the breath, but the moment we take our conscious focus off it, the automatic cycle returns. In modern society, this automatic cycle frequently consists of higher chest breathing, as opposed to deeper diaphragmatic breathing.

This is the type of breathing that takes place during the fight-or-flight response to extreme emotion and fear or during stress. This type of breathing is relatively shallow. As a result, it reduces our oxygen intake and fatigues the body-mind. When it becomes the normal breathing pattern, as it often does for adults and children, it places the body and mind in a constant state of stress.

Diaphragmatic breathing is quite the opposite. This is a breath that comes from deeper in the body, expanding the lungs fully and re-oxygenating our systems. This is the pattern we experience during calming meditation and deep trance. This is the type of breath we advise loved ones to take when they are upset. We tell them to "take a deep breath" and relax.

Through the conscious control of inhalation and exhalation, we can regulate our responses both to everyday reality and to our Otherworldly experiences. Children, including those with special needs, gain an ownership over their actions that they may not have believed possible before. The benefits to *pranayama* for children can range from an increase in memory and attention span to a reduction in uncontrolled or negative behaviors.

Through an ability to control the breath, children who tend toward emotional sensitivity can learn to step back from the situation, reestablish a calm and centered frame of mind, and then view things from a much more confident and expanded perspective. *Pranayama* is of great benefit in releasing fears and hurtful experiences before they are repressed and create more difficulties. We can take advantage of this energetic flow and release these energies before they become part of us.

This sounds very simple. All we need to do is pay attention and slow down our breathing when we want to. The truth is, it can take a considerable amount of practice. It can be difficult to pay attention to the breath all the time, especially for children. Once one's focus shifts, the habitual breathing pattern returns. Life does have a way of altering our focus. We get caught up in other things and forget all about our breathing. By the time we remember, it is often too late and we are feeling the effects of a return to habitual chest breathing.

The following breathing exercises are excellent for use with children. In the beginning, and particularly with children exhibiting Attention Deficit (Hyperactivity) Disorder or Obsessive Compulsive Disorder, it is recommended that you begin very simply. Start out by practicing simple breath awareness for a minute or less a few times a week. Increase the duration and frequency slowly. You will be able to observe what is comfortable and appropriate for your child. This is an excellent way to begin a homeschool day or to take a break when things get a bit intense.

Exercise: Diaphragmatic Breathing

Place your full attention on your breathing. Do not attempt to alter it, just observe for a few moments.

Now, slow your breathing. Count to three on each inhalation and again, on each exhalation. Breathe deeply, filling your lungs from the bottom first. Feel your diaphragm stretch and expand as your abdomen moves out. As you exhale, feel your abdomen contract as the breath leaves from the bottom of your lungs first.

Breathe into any areas of tension or pain. Feel your breath fill and relax these areas. With each breath, these feelings melt away, and you are filled with a sense of calm and comfort.

Once you feel comfortable performing this exercise, increase the count for inhalations and exhalations. Practice this several times a day, particularly when you are feeling stressed or are in pain.

Astrology and Your Child

All parents should be encouraged to have their children's astrological charts cast and interpreted by a professional with experience in reading for children. Astrology may be utilized as a tool for determining tendencies, karmic patterns and energies impacting one's life as well as for finding the best ways and times to communicate with certain individuals. This is where its greatest benefit lies as opposed to using it as a mere divination tool or an absolute pre-determiner of personality.

In these ways, astrology can be of great value to the homeschooling parent. Obviously, this can offer us a good overview into a child's personality, communication and perception styles, and life lessons. Through an astrological awareness of our children, we can gain a deeper understanding of what each child needs in different areas of life.

Depending on the placement of planets in houses and how they relate to each other, an astrological chart can provide a guide to children's physical, spiritual, and intellectual needs. This allows parents to see where children's strengths are and what areas they are likely to need some extra support in. Astrology offers insight into how children learn and how their creativity and self-expression may manifest.

Even more than this peek into who our children are, astrology can forewarn us about tendencies and energies that will enter our children's lives. The changing nature of the heavens impacts us in a myriad of ways. By exploring how current planetary positions relate to the planetary positions present at one's birth, we can prepare for these times as much as possible by knowing what areas of life are likely to be affected.

This allows us to understand their potential impact on our children and help our children to learn better from each experience. From an understanding of the transitory placement of the planets and asteroids, we have an idea of how long each phase will last. Sometimes just knowing that it won't last forever can be of immense help.

Special Needs Children

Many parents choose to home educate children with special emotional, mental, or physical needs for much the same reasons the rest of us home educate. However, they have additional concerns about the treatment and education their children receive in public schools due to their special conditions. Most of this chapter applies equally to these children, although sometimes in unique ways and with additional considerations.

I use the term "special needs" to encompass a wide variety of children. This broad term denotes those with behavioral challenges, such as Attention Deficit (Hyperactivity) Disorder, Asperger's Syndrome, and Obsessive-Compulsive Disorder. It includes children with physical challenges, such as Cerebral Palsy, Multiple Sclerosis, body organ failures, and life-threatening diseases such as leukemia. It also includes children with Down's Syndrome, Autism, and Fetal Alcohol Syndrome, among others. This term also incorporates those whom society would label as "gifted," although since each child has special gifts, I hesitate to use this term.

An ability to still the mind and body can be particularly important to these children. This provides them with a greater degree of control over Self and each success can result in increased self-confidence. Extra care and patience may be required with any of these children as they learn to attain these altered states.

Often relaxation can be more easily attained after some form of physical exercise. While exercise is not possible for all children, this can be particularly beneficial for ADD/ADHD children. In truth, exercise can be an invaluable component for any home educator.

Tense-Release forms of physical relaxation often work best, particularly with children who cannot engage in physical activity. In these methods, each body part is first tensed and then released in order to relax it. The obvious difference in feeling can make attaining the relaxation easier. As with any method, be aware of your child's attention span and interest. If it becomes a chore for them to focus on the exercise, stop and return to it later. This may also be used piecemeal to assist a child in relaxing a problem area of the physical body.

Exercise: Tense-Release

Begin in a safe and comfortable space where you will not be disturbed for at least 30 minutes. Experiment with starting at the toes and at the head to see which works best for your child.

Tense the muscles in your toes and then release them. Feel your toes relax.

Tense the muscles in your feet and then release them. Feel your feet relax.

Tense the muscles in your ankles and then release them. Feel your ankles relax.

Tense the muscles in your calves and then release them. Feel your calves relax.

Tense the muscles in your knees and then release them. Feel your knees relax.

Tense the muscles in your thighs and then release them. Feel your thighs relax.

Tense the muscles in your buttocks and then release them. Feel your buttocks relax.

Tense the muscles in your genitals and then release them. Feel your genitals relax.

Tense the muscles in your abdomen and then release them. Feel your abdomen relax.

Tense the muscles in your back and then release them. Feel your back relax.

Tense the muscles in your chest and then release them. Feel your chest relax.

Tense the muscles in your shoulders and then release them. Feel your shoulders relax.

Tense the muscles in your upper arms and then release them. Feel your upper arms relax.

Tense the muscles in your elbows and then release them. Feel your elbows relax.

Tense the muscles in your lower arms and then release them. Feel your lower arms relax.

Tense the muscles in your fingers and then release them. Feel your fingers relax.

Tense the muscles in your hands and then release them. Feel your hands relax.

Tense the muscles in your neck and then release them. Feel your neck relax.

Tense the muscles in your jaw and then release them. Feel your jaw relax.

Tense the muscles in your cheeks and then release them. Feel your cheeks relax.

Tense the muscles in your lips and then release them. Feel your lips relax.

Tense the muscles of your eyes and then release them. Feel your eyes relax.

Tense the muscles in your forehead and then release them. Feel your forehead relax.

Tense the muscles in your temples and then release them. Feel your temples relax.

Tense the muscles of your ears and then release them. Feel your ears relax.

Tense the muscles of your scalp and then release them. Feel your scalp relax.

Feel this relaxation sinking into your brain. Feel your brain relax.

Puberty

Puberty is often a time of upheaval for everyone in the family. Parents get sentimental over these very clear signs that their children really are becoming young adults. Some parents can respond with tears or through imposing additional social limitations on their children. Parents may also feel the connections they once had to their children have disappeared somehow.

Children are dealing with hormones. They are once again trying to balance independence and security while struggling to find their identities. They find they are suddenly somewhere between child and adult. They no longer fit into either category, and they alternate between trying to establish themselves as adults and wishing for the simplicity of childhood. This is a period of tremendous change that is manifesting on all levels of being.

Hormonal changes are related to the spiritual

changes occurring during adolescence. The entire energy field is undergoing another transformation and is relatively unstable at this time. Self-esteem is particularly vulnerable during this phase. Children are extremely sensitive as their chakras alternate between being wide open and closing down in defense. It is no wonder children often lose touch with what they are feeling in the chaos of emotional and energetic ups and downs.

For many children, this is when the chakras associated with the will and sexuality become most active. Vitality is at an all-time high and one's interest turns dramatically to sexual and emotional exploration. The experimentation of this time must be guided with wisdom. That is difficult to do when our children are subjected to the peer pressure and competition that are prevalent at most public schools.

Recall that as toddlers, children's energy fields stretched out toward the objects in their lives, often forming energetic cords, or attachments, to important objects that were perceived with ownership. During adolescence, these energetic cords are felt intensely. The loss of a friend, a lover, or one's status creates an energetic wound that can be experienced in a very similar way to a physical wound.

Adolescent homeschoolers may develop a strong need for peer interaction at these ages. Homeschool groups including children of all ages may not satisfy them anymore. Many home educating parents make an extra effort to form new groups or involve their teenage children in peer-specific outings and field trips.

Some home-educated children choose to attend

public school at these ages, even if only part-time. They may want more varied social interaction or they may prefer the competition of public school extracurricular activities, particularly school sports. These children are frequently quite capable of maintaining personal power by this age. While they are in the same type of energetic flux as other children in puberty, they have spent most of their younger years in deeply supportive environments.

Most of these children have been encouraged to be strong, independent individuals and not to simply follow the crowd. In ideal situations, they have been taught about their energy systems and how to ground or otherwise handle intense energies. These children know they are not alone and can come home whenever they choose. That tends to lend strength to school interactions.

Conversely, this is when some families choose to remove their children from public school, particularly during the middle school years. They do not appreciate the attitudes that are prevalent in school and they do not want their children to fall prey to a need to be in the "cool" crowd. These are families who act before their children lose personal power and end up with spiritual injury.

By puberty, the chakras are more rigid and well-defined. The belief systems are largely in place, and our filters are usually working quite well. But this does not mean that children no longer need adult guidance and protection. In fact, adolescents need this just as much now as they did when they were toddlers. We just need to be careful to offer it in ways that support mutual respect and recognize our children's new positions as young adults.

This is a good time for focused learning and in-depth exploration of advanced academic subjects. It is also an excellent time to involve interested children in a deeper immersion in creative and cultural pursuits. However, in general, this is not a good time to introduce advanced magical techniques. Certain traditions do introduce advanced elements around this time, but they have specific safeguards in place to counteract the energetic instability and openness of children in their tradition. This is not something to be taken lightly.

Once children are past puberty, things tend to settle down energetically, though they are still struggling to become individuals during these later years. As parents, we can support this in healthy ways or we can stifle it, requiring our children to rebel and fight back. The best thing we can do is to keep the lines of communication as open as possible while we give and expect respect.

Families who have raised their children with respect and honesty--and are continuing to do so--can expect fairly open communication and mutual respect to continue. This does not mean that children will want to be a parent's best friends or share everything. Parents need to learn to accept the reality that their children are individuals and are well on their way to becoming adults.

If you want to encourage a friendly relationship with your children later in life, you need to be supportive of the fact that they will now go forward and create their own lives. If you have established a healthy relationship, they will probably ask for guidance from time to time. But to see them creating the lives they choose as strong individuals is the best gift a parent can receive. This is what home education should result in, and we are all blessed in having shared the process.

Recommended Reading

Brennan, Barbara (1987) *Hands of Light.* Bantam Books

Madden, Kristin (2000) *Pagan Parenting.* Llewellyn

Chapter Three
The Curriculum Question

The use of a pre-packaged curriculum sounds ideal. You write a check and get the appropriate grade-level work for an entire school year in the mail. This can be a huge relief, especially for homeschooling parents who do have careers beyond home education. Children still get the freedom and one-on-one time, and parents get to save valuable time on planning.

It is true that boxed curricula work very well for some homeschoolers. But the majority find that these canned lessons create much of the same issues that public school does. Children do not always fit into the same grade level for every subject. If families are to truly follow these lesson plans for which they have paid so much money, they may lose the freedom for child-led education or the in-depth exploration of specific areas.

In addition, the pagan homeschooler who purchases a curriculum is still faced with finding appropriate ways to introduce spirituality and religion to their children. These aspects of pagan life are ideal learning opportunities. Children can learn about nearly every subject imaginable, simply through an exploration into the history, ritual, and science of paganism.

In my survey of pagan home educators, a little more than half consider themselves to be homeschoolers as opposed to unschoolers. Even among the homeschoolers, they tend to incorporate plenty of the unschooling philosophy into their lifestyle, particularly once they are past the first year of home educating.

Pagan paths lend themselves to an eclectic--and sometimes anarchistic- educational philosophy. Most of us came to our religions through doing a fair amount of searching. Most of us continue to read and self-educate within our chosen path and regarding other paths. Neopagan traditions are relatively new and they are dynamic, changing with each new voice that is added to the mix. Pagans often find a myriad of ways to learn more about the spiritual path they follow.

Pagans have largely rejected the status quo religions of modern Western society. We recognize the beauty of each individual expression of life. We tend to object to being told how to live, what to believe, and how to learn. As a result, pagan home educators often avoid the average boxed curricula and do not waste a great deal of time worrying about whether or not our children's education parallels that of mainstream society. In fact, many of us rejoice in the fact that our children have the opportunity to experience a unique educational experience.

Not one of those active homeschoolers responding to my survey follows a fully boxed curriculum. Several parents started out using them but discarded the whole idea after a year or two and now create their own course of study. Some supplement their own "curricula" with specific math or reading packages from commercial publishers. There are three main concerns with curricula among pagan home educators. The first is the cost. These programs are rarely cheap.

The second concern is that they are generally sold by grade level. That means that every subject in the package is designed for one grade level. This concern is not limited to pagan home educators. If your child is currently reading at a first grade level and doing math at a second grade level, much of what you have paid for will be unusable until a later date or will be an unnecessary review.

The third main issue is the fact that these are usually just like public school programs unless they are Christian curricula. There is no real belief in mythology, and the lessons are frequently devoid of spirituality. With only two exceptions[5], there is nothing available for purchase that uses or allows for the use of pagan spirituality as part of the learning format. Waldorf homeschooling curricula[6] are the next best option, and this system does not work for all families for a variety of reasons.

This is not to say that curricula do not work for a great many people. Some parents feel more comfortable knowing that their children are learning something created by experts. In many areas, home educators must be enrolled in a cover school[7] to be legal. Parents often doubt their ability to teach effectively. Even homeschooling veterans can have moments of doubt and fear.

Curricula provide a safe format within which to

teach. The preparation time for parents is very small, making education easier on parents. A few companies offer phonics or math as individual packages so parents do not need to buy all subjects for one grade level. There are also families who structure learning so that their children keep up with a specific grade level according to age. For these families, it works quite well. For those of you who do want to try out this option, the next section is designed to assist you in exploring your options and deciding what to try first.

How to Choose a Curriculum

The first step is to decide what type of curriculum you want. Internet programs are becoming more and more popular so that is an option to consider if you have a computer with Internet access and feel comfortable using it. Some companies offer both print and Internet courses.

Once the medium is determined, it is time to begin investigating the options. One way to get started is to request a catalog or visit the company's web site. Some companies offer a preview of the curriculum either by postal mail or online. You can take your time looking over the mission statement, course descriptions, and additional inclusions to the packet.

Start a checklist for each company and check off each item that is included. Which ones offer testing, worksheets, books, or manipulatives (like blocks)? Do they offer customer service or academic assistance? If so, are the hours convenient for you? Do they have additional assistance or activities on their web site?

Another way to decide what catalogs to request is to network. Ask other homeschoolers what their favorites are and if you can take a look at them. If there are stores that sell homeschool materials in your area, check to see what is available. You may be able to find some that have been used at a lesser cost. Ask the staff what sells best and what tends to come in "never used." Take advantage of homeschool conferences and curriculum fairs. Be warned that events listed as "conventions" are most likely fundamentalist Christian events, and they do ask that you sign a statement of religion before entering. There are often curricula for sale at these events, as well as plenty of networking opportunities.

When you have narrowed down your choices and listed all that is included for the price, take some time to decide what is important to you. Perhaps you don't need more manipulatives but want some type of academic assistance. You may decide that testing is not of great importance, but you want customer service to be readily available. Is the program accredited and what type of documentation or diplomas do they offer?

Are there religious undertones that you do not appreciate? Will it be fairly easy to integrate the spirituality you would like to include? If the best package for the price also comes with some recommendations from other homeschoolers, you have determined your curriculum.

Questionnaire: Choosing an Internet Program

- How reliable are your Internet provider and your computer? If your server goes down or your hard drive crashes, how much of an issue will that be for you?

- Is the program designed for homeschoolers or for classroom teachers? Ask how many homeschoolers have used the program and if there are testimonials available or clients whom you can speak with regarding the program. Of course, you will receive the glowing reports and talk to happy customers, but it is a place to start.

- Is the course on the Internet already and have the bugs been worked out? Be very cautious of companies that want you to pay up front for a program that will be available on the Web on a certain date. Consider the time involved in getting your money back if the company fails or if it takes significantly longer than expected to get it online.

- Are customer service, technical support, and any academic or other assistance included in the fee? Is specific contact information clearly identified? Consider testing reliability of and access to the contacts before buying.

- Are chat rooms and message boards available for students? Ask if you can visit them before buying. Even if you can't, you can certainly ask if they are available and how active they are.

- Are online tests included in the fee? How are they graded, and can they be customized?

- What is the fee schedule, and are there any hidden costs?

- Are all materials provided by the company and included in the fee?

- Will you be able to test a sample of the program before purchasing?

How to Create an Effective Curriculum

If you have decided against using boxed curricula or are using packaged programs for only certain subjects, you will need to consider how you want to structure your homeschool experience. If you are unschooling and are completely child-led, then there is no need to create a curriculum. But if you want more structure to your learning, you will base the form and materials on your particular approach to home education.

Many of us, at least in the beginning, follow some version of the traditional approach because that is what we know. It provides a definite framework and parallels the format in compulsory schools. This entails a specific number of hours to be devoted to formal education, using textbooks and worksheets. It generally follows the public school calendar as well. Some people will structure their days to closely approximate public school while others just use workbooks for key subjects.

There are other approaches based on the writings of education pioneers and psychologists, like Charlotte Mason and Dr. Raymond and Dorothy Moore. Unless you are really interested in educational philosophy, the names may be relatively unimportant because we create our own philosophies of living and educating as we go. Below I offer you another questionnaire to help pinpoint what is really important to you in an educational approach.

Questionnaire: Homeschool Approach

- Do your children respond best to a structured or loose environment?
- Do you have a specific number of hours and time frame in mind for homeschooling?
- Do you have an idea of what subjects you want to cover and how much of each you want to cover in one month or one year?
- How do your children learn best? Do they learn by listening, seeing, or doing? Are they very social or more introverted? How long is the attention span of each child?
- What are your children's strengths with regard to learning?
- What are your children interested in?
- Are you comfortable with incorporating play into your program? If so, how much?
- Do you feel that teaching academics at an early age is important? If so, how do your children respond to this?
- How much emphasis do you want to place on reading, math, science, ecology, history, art, music, etc.?
- Do you have access to a computer, television, or public library?
- Do you want to guide your children in developing a deep respect for all life and an acceptance regarding other cultures and religions?
- Do you want spirituality and/or religion to play a large role in your children's lives?
- What is your educational budget?

These questions will give a starting point from which you can more easily develop your own curriculum. Consider your responses when deciding how much structure you will incorporate and how many hours you want to schedule in one time block. The answers to this questionnaire will indicate where your preferences lie and how much religion you will include. This will also give you some insight into how effective workbooks will be as opposed to hands-on learning and field trips.

The answers to this questionnaire will also make for a much easier determination about what supplies you will need. Textbooks and workbooks can get rather expensive but so can high-tech or abundant educational toys. My family loves educational games and toys and we have partially solved the problem of expense by asking for specific gifts or gift certificates on holidays.

Another way to limit costs is to create your own games. This is a wonderful project for children to be involved in and can become an ideal assignment, incorporating a variety of subjects. Educational games can also be found on the Internet. Many can be played online and others can be printed out for use without a computer.

There are several ways to reduce the cost of books for home education. One of the best methods is to make use of the public library whenever possible. Get to know your library and the librarians. You might be surprised at what resources you find.

Older children using college level textbooks always have the option to sell books back to the college bookstore, though at a reduced rate. Many stores offer used textbooks. Some pagan communities, homeschool groups, and bookstores that cater to homeschoolers have lending libraries. These often include books that may not be obviously educational like textbooks are or may not be found at libraries, like books on paganism.

If you have an idea of what you want to cover in one month to one year, then you can plan the textbooks and other materials you will need for that course of study. In order to keep it inexpensive, shop around for the best prices and only buy what you are certain you will need. You can always run back to the flea market or store to pick up something else. If you have Internet access, bookmark or note the best web sites for free lesson plans, activities, and worksheets so you can easily return for more when you are ready.

I suggest you allow for a great deal of flexibility and not plan out each week a year in advance. There will be times that you want the week off or decide to follow a tangent for a couple of weeks, getting in-depth in a subject you did not anticipate. This is one of the joys of home education. We can do this without worrying that we are falling behind and won't meet the criteria to pass into the next grade by a certain date.

During a study of the solar system, Karl developed a fascination with the space shuttle and rockets. So we took a detour from focusing on the planets and moons themselves. We took a road trip to visit the space museum. We spent hours exploring the National Air and Space Administration (NASA) web site. We rented everything from small documentary films to big budget Hollywood films, anything that had to do with rockets, space shuttles, and NASA.

It took much longer than the planned three weeks

to complete that solar system study. We followed several diversions along the way. But a willingness to be flexible led to an in-depth understanding of the space program and a continuing fascination with astronomy for both of us. No, we didn't finish what we planned in the pre-determined time period. But we learned much more about a wider range of topics doing it our way.

Younger children are in a unique situation with regard to curricula. They tend to learn best through doing and touching. Their own unique styles of learning will usually show through this and these will become more evident as they grow older. But this emphasis on kinesthetic learning generally holds true, particularly with children under the age of seven. Energetically, these children are totally open to their world, and they soak it up like a sponge. In designing curricula for young children, this should be considered in order to design a healthy, balanced, and effective program.

Young children learn a tremendous amount through play and exploration. These are the ages to introduce the basic spirituality of religion. Young children respond well to talk of fairies, nature spirits, spirit guardians, and personal energy fields. This exploratory nature carries over into academics. Therefore, unschooling is highly effective at this age.

Children at these early ages love to investigate the outdoors. They possess an innate spiritual connection to the natural world, and we can use that to its greatest advantage in education. This is a perfect time to focus on stories and myths as well as the natural world. Reading to children and introducing them to computer skills is easy when we are telling stories and looking up beautiful pictures. The very young are not embarrassed to hug a tree or tell a flower they love it.

Many experts have suggested that formal education should be avoided at these ages. I disagree with such a general statement. Certainly young children learn a great deal from stories, artwork, play, dance and more at these ages. However, there are plenty of children who crave more formal learning as young as three years old. We should not deny these children their interests simply because an education "expert" says so.

I know several children between the ages of three and six who ask for formal homework. Our son started asking for homework at age four. He loves to learn in any format and will request worksheets or workbooks. When Karl was five years old, my mother asked me why he did not get a break on Memorial Day weekend. She visited to find him doing an addition worksheet that Sunday. I told her that he asked for it. Why would I refuse a request to learn?

Special Needs Curricula

Additional strategies may be required when designing a curriculum for children with special needs. The unique challenges and strengths of each condition must be incorporated into the program. If possible, interaction with children exhibiting similar conditions is recommended, even if this takes the form of a pen pal or email buddy.

You know your children best, and you understand their challenges. For the most part, necessary modifications are already part of your daily routine. You may already know how your children learn and respond without a conscious awareness of it. If you feel overwhelmed by the prospect of developing a curriculum for your special needs child, take a break from the educational mindset. Spend some time observing and playing with your child. Observe how the child plays alone and with others. Watch daily routines with more awareness than usual. You might be surprised at what you discover. It may be just what you need to develop confidence in yourself and your child.

As I said in the first chapter, parents have been known to allow their children to learn going up and down stairs or sitting with their heads on the floor. Highly functioning autistic children require a great deal of structure while some children with other conditions cannot tolerate much structure and need frequent play breaks. ADHD children tend to be kinesthetic learners, learning best through doing. With children like this, it is important to incorporate as much sensory learning as possible and offer a wide range of learning activities.

Some children will take considerably longer than others to grasp basic skills or abstract concepts. Some obsess over details unrelated to the learning at hand. Many children need to use language boards or sign language for communication, often slowing down the process.

If the need for behavioral modification is present, it often exists within the parent or family. All family members need to accept these situations without judgment. Families should work toward an honest release of any negative feelings regarding these conditions and parents' abilities to handle them. It is essential that we all find ways to behave so that we encourage self-confidence, positive self-image, and freedom of personal expression in each child.

Unit Studies

Unit studies focus on one topic for a period of time, usually one to six weeks. Parents with older children or those who have no challenges with maintaining focus for long periods of time will often schedule the unit to last five or six weeks but rarely longer than that. During this time, an in-depth exploration of the topic includes a great many academic subjects. This allows your family to choose a topic of interest and fully investigate it, learning as you go. Some experts suggest that significantly more learning occurs during integrated studies like this, as opposed to taking each educational subject independently.

This certainly allows for a deeper focus to develop as learning revolves around one topic. It can be seen as a type of immersion process, similar to foreign-exchange university language and cultural programs. It also can provide a helpful format, allowing you to educate children of different ages or learning styles simultaneously. Furthermore, children who have input into the topic of study are motivated to learn because it is something that already attracts them.

When our son first developed his interest in knights and King Arthur myths, we did a unit study on medieval times and legends. In no time, he was telling his friends about pages, squires, and knights. He explored a great deal of history, mythology, science (especially architecture), art, music, and more during a three-week unit study. He learned a lot through this study and developed a basic understanding of a variety of topics. About a year later, he did another medieval times study, with a slightly different focus. If he remains interested as he gets older, there is still plenty more to learn on this topic.

As pagan parents, unit studies can combine as much spirituality as we want. When Karl studied basic plant ecology, he learned of the medicinal, magickal, edible, and traditional uses of some local plants. We harvested sagebrush and tied our own smudge sticks. We made cottonwood drums. We blessed the garden together and talked of science and spirituality as though they were two sides of one integrated field, which we believe they are.

Unit studies can also be developed around specific pagan elements, such as magick or the festivals. When I organize children's rituals for our local community, I send participating parents links to relevant web sites to learn more about the associations of that season. Every year, Karl and I get into each festival in a little more depth as is appropriate for his age. I always plan for a short unit study around each festival.

One of my favorite aspects of unit studies is their value in demonstrating the interconnections of all things. As pagans, we can appreciate this from an energetic perspective. All things are connected on a spiritual level, and this manifests in physical reality. In real life, we integrate a variety of educational subjects within each project we do. Every challenge we meet is often handled with a combined approach.

When we shop, we use our abilities to read, make decisions, and often interact with other people. We perform basic mathematics, problem-solve, and may even include a bit of science, depending on what we are shopping for. As pagans, a challenge to create a new job is often met by a combination of hard work, networking, divination, and possibly spellwork. All of our skills are brought into play as we go through the daily process of living in this world.

Pagans recognize that life itself is a learning experience. Every person and situation presents us with the opportunity to learn and grow. Traditional schooling can limit this potential by requiring us to learn specific things at specific times. For example, compulsory school children may do math from ten to eleven in the morning and social studies from two to three in the afternoon. These subjects are mutually exclusive and once that class is finished, they often forget about it and move on. When school is over, they are finally free not to think at all. Clearly this is a broad generalization, but it does hold true in many cases.

Home education in general and unit studies in particular offer us the natural opportunity to view life holistically. In the course of a day, it may take some analysis to determine how much of the day was devoted to math or geography or chemistry because each aspect of real life involves a variety of "subjects." Learning in this way permits a broader perspective and a rare opportunity to see the pieces of the puzzle as one complete whole.

Home-educated children tend to possess an amazing ability to learn from everything in life, from taking a trip to the mechanic and stopping at a fast-food restaurant to helping to build shelves and cooking dinner. Certainly each of these situations teaches a specific subject or two, but what truly impresses me is that these children learn just as much about themselves, their Deities or spirit guides, and the world around them through these experiences.

How to Design Unit Studies

The creation of unit studies is a bit like creating mini-curricula throughout the year. It can be time intensive in the beginning to gather materials and decide on field trips, but older children can do a fair amount of that work as part of their education in research and planning. As they are drawn to a certain area within a topic, they can decide what methods and materials they want to use to investigate that further. For example, within a topic of ancient Greece, one child may be drawn to the Greek dramas and decide to write and act out a play. This will determine what materials are needed to write the play and put it on for the rest of the family.

In developing a unit study, try to allow your children to participate as much as is appropriate for their ages. They can learn a great deal even by simply observing as you plan the outline and gather materials. As you plan, create opportunities for your children to practice things like reading, writing, and mathematics as they explore other subjects within the main topic.

Once you have decided upon a topic, you will need to organize the study into an outline. This is not something that needs to be followed in order. It should also be fairly flexible. If you do not finish everything on your outline in the period of your study, leave it for next time. Chances are good that you will return to this study at some point in the future so you can feel comfortable allowing new directions to arise in the current study.

The outline is your basic format. It gives you the overall focus and any sub-topics you feel are important to cover. This can serve as a starting point for the creation of lesson plans for each week of the study. It also provides you with a reference to gauge your progress and to allow you to keep track of important aspects you want covered.

As you develop lesson plans for each day or each week of your study, there are several lists you will probably begin to compile. These lists can be an important time-saver during the course of the study, eliminating the need to search for references, activities, and more each day. When children need to wait for you to get organized before beginning their exploration, it can take much of the fun out of it. If you are anything like me, you do not want to have to get up at 4am each day to complete the search in time.

The first of these is usually the list of reference materials that go with each lesson plan. This will include relevant books, movies, games, software, and web sites. You may want to separate each medium into a list of its own for ease of use. Attempt to include both obviously educational materials along with those that have a large fun component. The fun ones will often instruct in subtle ways. They may also spark renewed interest in the topic.

Another important list notes all activities and field trips you may want to use for each lesson plan. You may want to include prices, directions, hours of availability, and contact phone numbers with each listing. Also include anything that is relevant and may be fun but does not readily fit into one of your predetermined lesson plans. You never know what may become applicable as you get into the study. You may also find that some of these are applicable to future unit studies. If you have all the information already on file, it saves time when you plan additional units.

Finally, some parents create a list of specific questions they feel should be answered through the study along with important spelling and vocabulary words their children should be learning. The inclusion and development of this list will depend on how structured and formal your homeschooling approach is. Some parents are very specific and may use this as the basis for testing. Others simply identify important concepts they want their children to begin to grasp while still others don't make any such list at all.

Homeschool Supplies

The most obvious home education supplies are probably paper, pens, highlighters, and notebook binders. Beyond that, your needs will depend largely on your approach to homeschooling, your budget, and the availability of external learning options in your area. The basics that everyone should consider having at home are listed below.

Before setting out to spend a considerable amount

of money on supplies, take the time to inventory what you already have at home. Look at your home with a new eye: that of the homeschool shopper. You may surprised at what the shopper in you can find to hold unique educational value among the everyday things in your home.

When Karl was learning to add and subtract, we started out using some colored glass balls. They were like mini-marbles that he could transfer back and forth between two bowls. At some point, he decided to forego the bowls, but these marbles kept rolling off the table so we switched to quartz crystals. He resonated with the crystals and had a lot of fun practicing math with them.

When Karl was learning about money, we kept our spare pennies in a plastic container for him to use for counting and for money games that we created. He got to keep the pennies (and later, quarters, dimes, and nickels) each time he did some work relating to money. Of course, my little Capricorn just loved that idea and learned quickly!

I now have an old dresser with drawers full of empty tissue boxes, toilet and paper towel cardboard rolls, leather scraps, shells, and a huge variety of art and craft supplies. During the Medieval unit study, we made him a helmet and armor out of dog bone and cereal boxes, feathers, and tin foil. During a geology study, he made his own sacred stones pouch out of scrap leather.

A current home inventory is likely to cut costs for any additional materials you may think you need. New or fancy materials are often unnecessary. Be wary of the need to purchase the biggest and most expensive. Your family's needs are likely to change from year to year. What worked for you last year may be sitting on a shelf next year. Unless you have a huge bank account, it is best to purchase what fits your current situation as opposed to what looks good.

When you know what you have, then you can start the list of what you need. At this point, knowing your approach and your children's unique learning styles will be very useful. Different approaches will have differing ideas regarding how and when to teach certain subjects. Some philosophies believe that reading and mathematics should not be taught until as late as second grade. Some approaches emphasize phonics before actual reading. Some will insist on the use of manipulatives (like Karl's math crystals) in learning mathematics.

In the beginning, you may not know what will work best. Once you do know, it may very well change. The best suggestion is to keep it as simple as you can and try to come up with your own worksheets, tests, and manipulatives. Try to choose books and programs that are not time intensive for you. Some teacher's guides can require a great deal of extra materials and preparation. Also look to see if the activities are based on classroom learning. These can require considerable time and thought to alter for one child or for a few children with very different levels and learning styles.

Access to libraries, zoos, museums, farms, and national parks, forests, or national monuments will add to your homeschooling experience. Library cards are usually free. However, admission to other places can add up to become a sizable portion your budget. Membership in museums or biological parks can often reduce the overall cost, but this option should be weighed heavily against a realistic expectation of use for any one facility. Getting together with other homeschoolers to take advantage of group rates is a good idea.

You might also consider your city or region with that new homeschool eye as well. You would be surprised at how many area businesses will offer tours and activities for free to homeschool groups. We have toured a local supermarket (and decorated cakes for free), the electrical company, a plant nursery, a goat farm, and a construction site, among others. We have enjoyed special rates on homeschool afternoon at a local theatre during appropriate plays. If you have the courage to ask, you may get some really interesting field trips for free.

Finally, to find out who offers an educator's discount, ask the managers at local businesses. If they do, tell them you are a home educator and be prepared to show homemade school identification or your state registration forms. Some of the larger chain bookstores offer ten to twenty percent off, though individual stores may be picky about what is "educational." Many art supply, video, music, office supply, science, computer, sporting goods, and even hardware stores will offer some discount to homeschoolers. I even convinced our state university's bookstore to offer homeschool discounts.

Below is a basic supply list to give you an idea of what most of us are using. You may go through a lot of paper so consider using recycled and reusing it as much as possible. This is where chalk and dry-erase boards become really valuable. We keep a stack of used paper with one clear side for reuse. Another great project is to keep some of the used papers and make your own paper from it.

Basic Supply List

- Art and craft supplies
- Building or construction games and supplies
- Calendar, monthly
- Chalkboard or dry-erase board
- Clock, large face
- Clock, digital
- Dictionary
- File cabinets or crates
- File folders
- Globe
- Library card
- Manipulatives: blocks, containers of marbles, pennies, or crystals, beads, etc.
- Maps: world, your country, your city or state (consider topographical and road maps; wall maps)
- Solar system
- Stickers (for tests, papers or projects)
- Table of elements
- Thesaurus

Recommended Reading

Armstrong, Thomas (1991) *Awakening Your Child's Natural Genius: Enhancing Curiosity, Creativity, and Learning Ability.* J P Tarcher

Hirsch, E.D. Core Knowledge Series (*What Your Kindergartener Needs to Know...*) Delta Pub.

Madden, Kristin (2000) *Pagan Parenting.* Llewellyn.

Phillips, Debora and Fred Bernstein (1991) *How to Give Your Child a Great Self-Image.* Plume

Reed, Donn (1994) *The Home School Source Book.* Brook Farm Books.

Rupp, Rebecca (2000) *Home Learning Year by Year: How to Design a Homeschool Curriculum from Pre-school Through High School.* Three Rivers Press

Tobias, Cynthia Ulrich and Carol Funk (1997) *Bringing Out the Best in Your Child: 80 Ways to Focus on Every Kid's Strengths.* Servant Publications

Resources

Pagan

Goddess Moon Circles Academy
Box 129
Madras, OR 97741-0029
541-546-6108
gmcaenroll@goddessmooncirclesacademy.org
http://www.goddessmooncirclesacademy.org

Lytl Witch Pagan Homeschooling Curriculum
online curriculum
http://www.lytlwytch.com/paganhomeschoolingcurriculum.shtml

Sacred Grove Academy (Alabama only)
C/o Church of the Spiral Tree

PO Box 186
Auburn, AL 36831-0186
Homeschool@sacredgroveacademy.org
http://www.sacredgroveacademy.org

General

Alger Learning Center
national distance learning program; supports unschooling
121 Alder Dr.
Sedro-Woolley, WA 98284
800-595-2630
orion@nas.com
http://www.independent-learning.com

American School
high school courses
2200 East 170th St
Lansing, IL 60438
800-531-9268/708-418-2800

Calvert School
K-8 curriculum
105 Tuscany Rd
Baltimore, MD 21210
410-243-6030/410-366-0674
inquiry@calvertschool.org
http://www.calvertschool.org

Classroom Direct
Educational supplies

PO Box 830677
Birmingham, AL 35283-0677
800-599-3040
Fax 800-628-6250
http://www.classroomdirect.com

Clonlara School Home Based Education Program
programs for all grades; CompuHigh through the Internet
1289 Jewett St
Ann Arbor, MI 48104
734-769-4515
Clonlara@delphi.com
http://www.clonlara.org

Live Education!
Waldorf Curricula
P.O. Box 306
Aptos, CA, 95001
831-457-4243
info@live-education.com

Massachusetts Institute of Technology
OpenCourseWare
materials for nearly all MIT courses available free via Internet
by the end of the pilot program (2001-2003)
http://web.mit.edu/newsoffice/nr/2001/ocw-facts.html

Math-U-See
mathematics curricula
888-854-MATH (6284)

In Canada 1-800-255-6654
http://www.mathusee.com/index.html

Oak Meadow
cover school for all ages, including outside the USA
PO Box 740
Putney, VT 05346
802-387-2021
Fax: 802-387-5108
oms@oakmeadow.com

Saxon Publishers, Inc.
math and phonics for pre-K through 12
2450 John Saxon Blvd.
Norman, OK 73071
800-284-7019
Fax: 405-360-4205
info@saxonpub.com
http://www1.saxonpub.com/index.html

The Education Connection
books, games, and more
PO Box 910367
St George, UT 84791
800-863-3828/35-656-01112
catalog@educationconnection.com
http://www.educationconnection.com

Timberdoodle Company
miscellaneous homeschool materials
E. 1510 Spencer Lake Road
Shelton, WA 98584

360-426-0672
Fax 800-478-0672
mailbag@timberdoodle.com
http://www.timberdoodle.com

World Book
World Book International's Typical Course of Study: free
Internet or print
4788 Hwy 3775
Ft. Worth, TX 76116
800-967-5325
http://www.worldbook.com/ptrc/html/fp.htm

Zephyr Press
multiple intelligence books, games, and more
3316 N. Chapel Avenue
Tucson, AZ 85716
520-322-5090/800-232-2187
Fax 520-323-9402
zephyrpress@zephyrpress.com
http://www.zephyrpress.com

Internet Only General

Content Standards
http://www.gomilpitas.com/homeschooling/materials/
Content.htm

DiscoverySchool.com
Discovery channel lessons plans and more
http://school.discovery.com/

Dositey.com
free worksheets
http://www.dositey.com/index.html

Freeworksheets.com
http://www.schoolexpress.com/fws/default.asp

SchoolExpress.com
free worksheets, online activities, and online store
http://www.schoolexpress.com/default.asp

TV Watch
links to educational tv shows and available activities/ lesson plans
http://www.quailhaven.com/hsboard/tvwatch.htm

Vegsource.com
used curricula
http://www.vegsource.com/homeschool/

Chapter Four
Networking

Have you ever known someone that seemingly held an incredible amount of useful knowledge and whatever they didn't know, they could come up with at lightning speed? That person was most likely a great networker. Some people have an innate ability to get information and persuade other people to help them in a variety of ways. Knowledge and opportunities appear to flow easily to these people. It really is a gift and one that we all could benefit from developing.

Networking can be an important part of any homeschooler's journey. Learning to be an effective networker can provide you with a vast array of social and educational opportunities. Speaking with a wide variety of people can help you to stay current with state and local legislation or other news of interest to home educators. Effective networking can help you find the right homeschool group and get invitations to new groups or private educational events. It can help you find the best materials at the lowest prices and get an opportunity to preview materials before purchasing.

Pagan Networking

The ability to network can be particularly valuable for pagans since the majority of other homeschoolers you are likely to come in contact with are either Christian or predominantly secular. If you want interaction with other pagan families or information about including spirituality into your studies, you need to find other pagan homeschoolers.

Unfortunately in some areas, face-to-face access to other pagans does not exist. If it does, it may be extremely limited. Often in these places, pagan families need to be careful about what they share and with whom regarding spiritual beliefs and practices. They may have very realistic fears of losing jobs, facing harassment, or dealing with custody battles over their children. The Internet has become a lifesaver for these and many other pagan parents.

A search on Yahoo Groups at the end of 2001 for "pagan homeschooling" found thirty-three email lists, including several that are specific to a U.S. state or region of the world. I have started a Yahoo group specifically for families looking to network or connect with other families:

http://groups.yahoo.com/group/
PaganParentNetworking

There are also lists for pagan teens and children who are homeschooled. Several personal web sites and other groups host additional lists and message boards. Most parents in my survey found support and friends online. Those without a personal computer often use public libraries for Internet access.

I met some of my very best friends online. I connected with my pagan homeschool groups and the local pagan community through email lists. I make great use of the Internet for educational purposes, both as a homeschooler and as a writer. Karl started using the computer at three years old, and he is quite skilled at it now. A few months ago, I even found him teaching his grandmother a few things. It is such a valuable resource that I recommend finding a library or friend who will allow some access if you do not have your own computer.

If you are already in touch with a pagan community, this is a great opportunity to develop networking skills in a more comfortable arena and discover some great information along the way. You may be surprised at the areas of expertise that exist within your own community. In various pagan communities I have been a part of, there have been politicians, doctors and nurses, astroarcheologists, astronomers, lawyers, authors, actors, ecologists, engineers, architects, and many more. I have known people with a special interest in physics, geology, botany, sculpting, drum making, history, and languages, among other fields. When I look beyond pagan communities, this list grows exponentially.

A pagan community can also be a great source of like-minded socialization for you and your children. Whether or not there are other children involved, everyone benefits from having others with similar beliefs to interact with from time to time. If other pagan children are part of that group, that is even better.

If you do not have access to a computer or a community, try pagan and New Age print publications. Several of these provide space for networking and personal ads. While you do need to be cautious when meeting anyone through ads or computers, they are worth investigating. Local groups may post ads for open rituals or potlucks. With some discernment, you may connect with some wonderful people in this way. My husband and I made contact with the pagan communities soon after moving to upstate New York and Connecticut through *Circle* magazine and local newsletters.

Metaphysical Centers and Bookstores

While I spend hours each day on the computer and even shop online fairly frequently, I believe strongly in supporting local booksellers and metaphysical centers. One reason is because of their value to the networker. These shops often have bulletin boards where people can post local groups, events, and other information. These can be wonderful places to start the search for people and information.

But more than that, the people who own and work for these stores are great resources. They know their clientele and tend to keep up with global and local happenings in any field of interest to that clientele. They have readers, healing practitioners, teachers, and craftspeople coming to them all the time. Quite often these people have lived in the area for some time and are in touch with a vast array of communities.

The other great thing about these people is that they are already in the business of answering questions and assisting people. In general, they welcome questions and would probably be flattered that you consider them a valuable resource. Don't be shy. Make an attempt to get to know the people in your area and don't limit it to pagan or metaphysical centers. In networking with all kinds of people, you may find like-minded folk in unexpected places. Just as importantly, you will begin to develop a diverse web of possibility for yourself and your children.

Below is an outline of networking basics. These are suggestions on where to begin and how to proceed. For this list to be truly useful for you, you must experiment with it. Find out what works best for you and where your greatest strengths are. Allow yourself to be open to alternative possibilities that arise through this testing. We each network in our own unique ways. The most effective networkers don't worry about perceived mistakes. They learn from every experience and continually revise their own personal list of basics.

Networking Basics

- Decide what specific and general information you need. Be clear and develop some initial questions based on what you hope to find. While some great additional ideas are often sparked by networking, don't lose your focus and get overwhelmed.
- Take every opportunity to talk to people and ask your questions. Ask other homeschoolers, your neighbors, store owners, and people on the grocery line. Ask people for their sources

or for their reasons for giving the advice they do.

- Consider how reliable or experienced each person is. Learn to trust your intuition about people, without falling prey to personal judgments.
- Follow up on leads and go to the source whenever possible. For example, if you want information regarding a particular college, ask the relevant department at that college. If you want to know what math program is best, ask other homeschoolers for their opinions but also ask the company if you can preview the materials yourself. Keep in mind that your experience may differ from that of other homeschoolers.
- Don't give up! If you feel you are not getting anywhere, revise your focus or find alternative sources. Persistence and creativity will eventually pay off.

In number two of the above list, I suggest taking every opportunity to ask other people. This is excellent advice because you never know who will hold the key to what you need. However, it is true that you are more likely to find your answers with certain people and places than others. Obviously, the best way to begin is to consider where the experts are. Another way is to start at a place where a wide variety of information can found.

Libraries

I do not know a home educator who does not use the public library, at least on occasion, unless they do not have ready access to one. Many homeschoolers spend a considerable amount of time in their local libraries. Those fortunate enough to have a college or university nearby never fail to take advantage of the campus library, especially with older children and teenagers at home.

Libraries hold a wealth of information and it is not all contained in the books on the shelves. Librarians are not only highly skilled at finding worthwhile information among the rows and rows of literature, they have often been trained in Internet research. Furthermore, they keep up with community events and groups, particularly educational ones. They may already know a great deal about homeschooling in your area.

Librarians are the ones to ask about inter-library loans, which are sadly underutilized because many people do not know about them. These are valuable when your local library system does not have what you need. You can sometimes check on textbooks and curricula in this way. Often public libraries will have special agreements with other libraries, including university libraries, to loan materials for free. Other loans may entail a small fee. In any event, you will need to request an Inter-Library Loan form from the librarian.

Library web sites can contain vast amounts of information and links to other informative sites. In some areas, you can hold or renew books online. Several library systems offer homework help or reference assistance online. Many places list their special programs and storytimes on their web sites. Karl and I applied for our library cards online, and they were mailed to us within a week.

Another resource that may be found at libraries is a community information section. This is usually placed near the door, but it may be located at relevant areas around the library. For example, children's programs are frequently posted in the children's book section. These community sections consist of bulletin boards, tables, and displays or any information that may be of interest to the community served by that library.

Park and recreation materials are often placed in these sections, along with notes on registration dates and places for organized sports. Special interest clubs, like model airplane or chess clubs, music and drama groups, and government-sponsored programs will have brochures or posters present here. Many areas have community college and university catalogs present, along with free magazines listing area activities. Several places have magazines specific to children's events and some even have homeschool publications available.

Public Schools and Colleges

Potentially valuable resources can also be found in compulsory schools and colleges. These resources are teachers, and they can be of great help in choosing the best homeschool supplies and resources, if you can get them to talk to you.

Experienced teachers have probably done most

of the searching you are doing right now. They know where to get good supplies and how much things cost. They have resources that provide them with additional ideas for activities and lesson plans.

This can be a tricky area in which to network. If you know teachers personally, then things are relatively easy. Many teachers and teacher-assistants are happy to help interested parents and students provided the time investment for them is small. But the truth is, teachers and some college professors are often overworked and underpaid. They can have little time available to help anyone not directly involved in their current classrooms. It is also unfortunately true that some school districts and individual teachers are hostile towards homeschoolers for a variety of reasons including lack of education and misinformation.

It is in everyone's best interests if you can bypass any potential discomfort and develop a working relationship with the schools. School officials will benefit from greater understanding of home education and seeing your dedication first-hand. Other home educators will thank you for your courage and your ability to forge some early connections that may pave the way for future interactions. If you are able to be open about your pagan beliefs, you have created yet another opportunity to handle misconceptions. You and your children will gain valuable information and possibly some new contacts that may be of benefit in the long-term for additional questions or even letters of recommendation someday.

Raising Effective Networkers

Teaching children to network is part of guiding them to take control of their own lives. When children learn this skill from parents and develop their own networking abilities, they hold a basic yet powerful tool for life. Children who learn to network effectively can access any information they need. They can become experts at finding unique ways to get the opportunities they want. Doors open for these children that may not for those who never learn to network.

Through the process of networking, children develop investigative and research abilities that will serve them in countless ways. They learn to think critically, to do literature searches, to evaluate sources and information, and to succeed in a wide variety of educational and career paths. There are few other things we can teach that will have such deep and far-reaching value for our children.

Networking is a skill that must be practiced to fully develop. You can sit down with your children and explain the concept. You can have them review the Networking Basics list in this chapter. You can make up lists of people and places that might prove valuable in your search. But none of these activities will teach you to read people, follow intuition, or overcome shyness. All these are necessary components in good networking.

The best way for children to develop these abilities and learn to network well is to be present and included when a parent networks. Early on, just let them watch what you do and how you do it. If they are old enough to understand, explain to them what you are doing and why. Think out loud at home or in the car and allow them to observe the process through both your words and actions.

When you feel they are ready, ask them to be fully present while you network. Talk about the experience in more depth during and afterward. Encourage them to ask questions and be prepared to ask some leading ones yourself. Guide them to think about what people you spoke with and what other resources you utilized. Have your children critique the questions you asked and how you opened or directed the conversation. Ask them how they would have done it differently.

After learning through your example, your children need to actually do it to take that learning to another level. They can begin at home with a simple task that can be accomplished through talking to family members and looking at your home with that Homeschool Eye I mentioned earlier. See what they come up with and discuss it as you would any educational assignment or any life event that may arise.

Encourage your children to keep a networking journal. You may even choose to use this for your own purposes. One blank page is included at the end of this chapter. You may print it out and use it as is or use it as a guideline for creating your own. The journal provides an opportunity to document what they wanted to accomplish, how they devised the plan, what they did, and any successes or problems encountered. As time goes on, they can refer back and learn from mistakes or refine things that worked well.

The journal includes a question about what made

you uncomfortable. This is an important question, and one that will offer many insights. It is possible that a feeling of discomfort might be created by an intuition that this lead will not be of value or that the person you are speaking with is uncomfortable with your questions or demeanor. It is also a good possibility that discomfort indicates a shyness or self-consciousness interacting with others in this manner. It might also be a sign that on some level you are aware something you are doing is not right for you or unethical in some way.

Each of these possibilities should be examined whenever discomfort arises. Until you gain enough self-knowledge to know immediately why you feel anything, you cannot fully trust your own intuition about these things. Self-knowledge leads to self-confidence, and that is an important quality to cultivate.

Self-knowledge Meditation

Count down from ten to one, breathing slowly and deeply. Periodically, tell yourself you are getting more relaxed and centered. At the count of one, tell yourself you are completely relaxed and centered and perfectly safe in this state of mind.

Focus your attention on your body. Breathe deeply and recall the memory of what made you uncomfortable. How does this memory affect you? Where in your body or mind do you feel the discomfort?

Allow your breathing to take you into that area of your body-mind. See it before you and follow the feeling of discomfort into its center. What do you find there? Acknowledge any images, thoughts or feelings that come up for you.

Ask your Higher Self or your spirit guides for additional guidance. Ask them to show you what you need to know regarding the discomfort you felt and any images you have become aware of. Ask them what you need to learn from this.

Ask that the least emotionally charged of those images and feelings come forward. Look deeply into the core of what comes up. Where did this come from and how does it relate to your experience? What does it have to teach you?

Reach out and hold this image. See the both of you fill with light. Feel yourself filling with strength as the image is transformed from something uncomfortable into something productive. Be aware of how it changes to become something valuable as it integrates into your being.

Continue this process until you have either had enough for this session or have transformed and integrated all that came up.

Thank your Self and your guides for their blessings and guidance in this process.

Count yourself back up from one to ten, reminding yourself periodically that you are coming up to normal awareness. At the count of ten, tell yourself that you are back in normal awareness and that you are stronger than before. Say that you feel wonderful and are full of light. State with intent that with each passing day, you gain more self-knowledge and insight into yourself.

This meditation is an excellent first step in developing the confidence necessary to take control of your own life experience. As confidence grows, you are likely to be more comfortable in anything that you need to do, including networking. You can ask your Deities and spirit guides to help in this pursuit. Beyond that, the best way to achieve self-confidence is to create your own successes and gain experience.

As parents, you can help your children to create early networking successes that will lead to increased effectiveness and self-confidence. This is accomplished through setting realistic goals and offering the necessary support for their successful completion. You can also do this by gradually increasing the independence and difficulty with which your children network.

Some children will take to it naturally and strike out on their own whether you encourage them to or not. Other children may need help focusing or gaining the confidence to speak to potential resources. But whether your children are natural networkers or not, you can learn much about yourself and your children by guiding them in developing this valuable skill.

Networking Journal

Date:

Objective/What I want to find out:

Overview of my plan:

People I spoke with **Results**

Books I looked at **Results**

Web sites checked **Results**

Other resources used   **Results**

Did this accomplish my goal?

If not, what are my next steps?

What worked best?

What did not work?

What made me uncomfortable?

Chapter Five
The Online Connection

What books used to bring to the masses, the Internet often does now. All you need to do is search the appropriate words or follow interesting links, and you have access to a virtual universe of information, photos, games, rituals, and potential friends. With a computer and a modem, you can escape into stories, legends, ancient sites, and modern fantasies.

The Internet has become one of the biggest and most important resources for pagans, particularly homeschoolers. It is an efficient means of contacting a large number of people and finding those with similar interests among the many. The fact that a web site is accessible twenty-four hours each day for as long as the service provider is working properly allows for it to be seen by people around the world whenever they happen to be online. The Internet makes it possible for pagans to remain firmly in the closet if they so desire while they surf pagan sites and interact with other pagans in complete anonymity. The value of this cannot be understated.

As I wrote earlier, there are areas of the world where pagans cannot comfortably be open about their spiritual beliefs and practices. In some places, parents have valid concerns for the safety and emotional well-being of their families if anyone were to discover that they are pagan. Pagan homeschoolers have been harassed and forced to justify their religion to school districts, neighborhoods, and even family members. In situations like this, the ability to connect with other pagan home educators can become a lifeline for a family.

Even for those of us who are open about our spiritual practices, the Internet provides access to a wide range of information on pagan paths, opinions, rituals, and scholarly research. Through the Web, we can interact with groups and individuals whom we might not otherwise have the opportunity to communicate with or even know about. It saves time and often money. It connects us with like-minded people with whom we can share, vent, discuss, support, and laugh.

Obviously, parents need to maintain an awareness of their children's Internet habits. You do not need to regulate or monitor every communication. Most email lists for pagan children, parents, and homeschoolers are moderated and are very safe from predators. However, predators- whether they are unethical salespeople or far worse--do exist, and we all need to be aware of this.

It is important to teach children Internet safety along with computer and research skills. Just as they need to know not to get into strangers' cars, they also need to know what to be aware of and stay away from while they are online. In order to ease their transition into the world of Internet communications and prevent them from appearing like a rank beginner to those who might offer to "help," parents should also teach them how to use email, instant messaging services, chat rooms, and search engines correctly. Parents might also give children a basic list of netiquette, or appropriate email behavior.

Early on, you should plan to discuss and set rules for Internet usage as a family. Decide what is going to work best for everyone, particularly if you have only one computer. If disagreements arise, and they are likely to, parents need to take control and make strong but reasonable decisions. These rules can include anything from how many hours each person can spend online and how late the computer can be on to if files can be downloaded or what sites are inappropriate.

Some experts advise parents to monitor their children's emails and check on the web sites they visit. Most of the pagan parents I know feel this is an unnecessary invasion of privacy unless there is a history of problems with Internet usage. Many pagan parents object to policing their children by reading all their emails and quizzing them on who they are communicating with, unless there is a valid reason to do so.

It is a good idea simply to focus on clear and open communication with children unless a realistic problem is expected to arise. In this way, lines of communication can remain open and safe, so that families can discuss concerns and potential problems things together. Children should not be afraid to go to parents with something that makes them uncomfortable, and the perceived need to keep secrets can spell trouble for the future. The use of personal passwords is up to you, but if a family maintains trust and respect, there should be no need for them.

Basic Internet Safety for Kids

- Do not open email or respond to messages from anyone you do not know.
- Do not open file attachments without a parent's permission.
- If you get any e-mail or instant message that makes you uncomfortable, show it to your parents.

Basic Netiquette

- Do not use all capital letters. This is perceived as shouting and is both unnecessary and annoying to readers.
- Stay on topic if replying to an email list or message board. Off-topic or personal conversations should be taken to private email.
- If you get into an argument with someone, agree to disagree and let it go. Do not risk harassment by pursuing the individual. If you are being harassed, report it to your service provider (children should inform their parents).
- Keep in mind that tone of voice and facial expressions are not part of email communications. It can be difficult to tell if a person is kidding. Until you learn all the emoticons[8] and acronyms[9] used in this type of commu-

nication, enclose your intention in parentheses or asterisks if it might be misunderstood[10].

- Be careful when choosing a screen name or online ID. Children, in particular, should not use their full names or real last names. They should also not use a name that may have sexual connotations.

The Internet is a tremendously valuable resource when used appropriately and intelligently. It allows parents and children to expand their horizons and their social interactions in a predominantly safe space. With some education and continuing discussion, you and your children can benefit in a multitude of ways, simply by having access to a computer and a modem.

Below I describe the more common resource types that can be found on the Internet. Each of these is unique and some people tend to prefer some over others. Personally, I avoid chat rooms but love email lists. I love the freedom to reply when I have the time and the ability to consider what I want to say. I know plenty of people who want direct, real-time connections with others so they frequent chat rooms.

I will offer one final note of caution. Be aware that a web site can be published on the Internet by anyone. What you read on the Web is not necessarily true or accurate. People may not be what they appear to be. It is important not to accept blindly each piece of information you find. Test the information to see if it holds up to scrutiny. Ask others for their opinions about a certain web site or individual. Just because a site gets a lot of visitors or has been around for a year or two does not mean that it is valuable.

Email Lists

Email lists and newsgroups are group emails. Sometimes they are run by individuals or stores and other times they go through one of the online organizations that provide space and a variety of options for these groups. Email lists in particular have become very popular in recent years. These are groups that are specific to an area of the country or a certain lifestyle, hobby, or interest. People can join public groups freely. As long as they abide by the rules of the list, they are welcome to stay and either observe or participate in discussions for as long as they like.

There are a great many pagan parenting and pagan homeschooling email lists available. Most of the parents in my survey connected with local groups or found supportive friends through these lists. For many of these families, email was their only connection to other pagan homeschoolers. For some, it was their only connection to other pagans, homeschooling or not.

The existence of email lists for kids and teens is relatively new. This is a wonderful development in that it provides a social opportunity for children who might not otherwise have pagan peers to interact with. Even for those children who benefit from a local community, email can open up a whole new world of friends, support systems, and networking. Some children who meet friends at festival gatherings exchange email addresses and keep in touch through the rest of the year via email.

Web Sites

    I doubt anyone knows for certain just how many web sites exist on the World Wide Web. Each day more are being published and some are being deleted. You can find just about anything you might be interested in through a simple Web search.

    The ever-increasing number of pagan web sites, particularly those dedicated to parenting and home education are a wonderful resource for the pagan homeschooler. Most of us want to know what other pagan parents are doing and how they are introducing concepts or creating rituals for their children. We often want ideas to play with in our own families. The creators of these sites offer all this and more.

    These web site designers provide us with an insight into the pagan family in its many forms. They discuss their successes and failures along with what they are experimenting with at any given time. They share their poetry, stories, ideas, arts, and crafts with us. They also review books, movies, games, and more so we have a better idea of what to expect if we are considering making a purchase.

    Beyond the pagan realm, the abundance of strictly secular educational web sites is truly astounding. States and countries have their own educational sites. Most large public school districts have an amazing array of information on their sites. Museums, zoos, aquariums, and teaching facilities all are likely to have web sites. Homeschool curriculum publishers and cover schools are frequently online as are the publishers of metaphysical and educational books.

A great many of these sites provide teacher and student pages within the site. These may contain lesson plans, activities, worksheets, and more. Some of these are interactive for use online. Others can be printed for use offline.

Ezines

The ezines, or electronic magazines, are a relatively new development among pagan home educators. Some of the secular ones have been around for quite some time. They are a wonderful resource for all of us. Along with the usual web sites, these ezines feature volunteer writers who willingly share their words and experiences so that the rest of us need not be forced to start blindly at the beginning. Occasionally, you will find an article from a well-known pagan or home educating author among the other offerings on web sites and ezines. This arena has great potential for the future and is another possible cost saver for the home educating family.

Online Classes

Also fairly new on the Internet are online curricula, individual courses, and even college materials. Many adults are already taking advantage of Internet course offerings and online universities, but few people realize that there are a wide variety of classes available online for children of all ages as well. Some online universities will permit teens to take college courses with parental permission. Many cover schools and some curriculum providers offer an online supplement to their course work.

Because of the concerns regarding public school, some school systems are offering virtual schools to select students. These programs offer regular and advanced school classes along with test preparation services, college preparation assistance, and more. Depending on funding, these are not always limited to students in outlying, rural areas.

The Massachusetts Institute of Technology released a decision in April of 2001[11] regarding the offering of nearly all MIT course information over the Internet. A pilot program is planned for completion in 2003, after which an estimated 500 courses will be available online. This is a wonderful precedent and may be very beneficial for homeschooled teens.

These kinds of programs are going to change the face of education for the future. They do not take the place of any other form of education, but they certainly have great potential for additional or supplemental learning without the ecological and financial expense of paper, books, and mailing. The availability of alternative courses and online pagan curricula will make it much easier for home educators who want this type of supplement to their children's academics but can't take the chance at being "Out" in their local areas.

The creators of these sites and email lists are individuals who have become extremely talented at web design and web publishing. Every time I surf the Web, I am amazed at the incredible designs and information that are available from my fellow pagans. Some sites are so packed with information that I wonder where the webmaster or webmistress found the time. Often these are people with jobs just like the rest of us who volunteer their time and ability to bring the best to a global pagan community. Each and every one, no matter how small the site, deserves our congratulations and thanks.

By now it should be clear that the Internet is an incredible resource for the pagan home educator. Many of the benefits of this technology are discussed throughout this book. Anyone with a rudimentary understanding of the Internet and search engines can access free worksheets, lesson plans, calendars of events and educational television programs, and learning games. This technology allows us to preview curricula and distance learning programs and to order a vast array of materials without ever leaving home. It frequently contains the most up-to-date news, research, theories, and events.

The problem with creating in-print lists of good Internet sites is the changeable nature of the medium. By the time a book goes to print there is a possibility that at least some of the listed resources will no longer exist. It is for that reason that I choose to list only those that are really excellent and, in most cases, have been around for quite some time. Anyone checking these sites, participating in email lists, and doing their own Internet searching is bound to find all the new sites eventually. I must add that I will probably miss some good sites simply because I have not yet hit upon them in my own search. To those webmasters, I offer my apologies.

Pagan Homeschool Web Sites

Circle Sanctuary
http://www.circlesanctuary.com

dmoz Open Directory Project: Pagan Homeschooling Links
http://dmoz.org/Society/Religion_and_Spirituality/Pagan/Parenting/Homeschooling/

Goddess Moon Circles Pagan Homeschooling
http://www.goddessmoon.org/pagan.html

Jon's Homeschool Resource Page: Pagan
http://www.midnightbeach.com/hs/UniFrame.html?JumpBar="Web_Pages.j.html"&Main="/hs/pagan.htm"

Lytl Wytch Pagan Family Pages
http://www.lytlwytch.com/

MamaWitch
Pagan Homeschool Page
http://www.homestead.com/barbooch/PaganHomeschool~ns4.html

Mom Madden's Place
http://hometown.aol.com/mommadden/welcome.html

PaganParenting.com
http://www.paganparenting.com/

Pagan Parenting Page
http://paganparenting.net/information/homeschooling.html

Starry Sky Studio Unschool
http://www.angelfire.com/nm/starrysky/unschool.html

WitchyWorks Pagan Kids Pages
http://www.witchyworks.com/pagankids/

General Homeschool Web Sites

A to Z's Home's Cool
http://www.gomilpitas.com/homeschooling//

Homeschooling Today Online
http://www.homeschooltoday.com/home.htm

Homeschool World
http://www.home-school.com/

Omniseek Homeschool
http://www.omniseek.com/dir/Education/Home+Schooling

Ezines

Acorns: Pagan Homeschool Newsletter
http://members.tripod.com/acorns3/

Merry Begot
http://www.merrybegot.homestead.com/

Educational Resources

General

abcteach
http://abcteach.com/index.html

Activities for Kids
http://www.activitiesforkids.com/teacher.htm

Ask Eric – Lesson Plans
http://ericir.syr.edu/Virtual/Lessons/index.shtml#Search

A to Z Home's Cool
http://www.gomilpitas.com/homeschooling/

Dositey.com
http://www.dositey.com/index.html

Homeschool Associates
http://www.homeschoolassociates.com/index.mv

Houghton Mifflin Education Place
http://www.eduplace.com/search/activity.html

LearningPage.com – Sites for Teachers
http://www.sitesforteachers.com/

Quia
http://www.quia.com/index.html

RHL School
http://www.rhlschool.com/

Resources by Subject (Education Resource Center – NASA Langley)
http://www.vasc.org/erc/resources_at_trc.html

SchoolExpress.com
http://www.schoolexpress.com/

Sites for Teachers
http://www.sitesforteachers.com/

Young Minds Homeschool
http://donnayoung.org/

World Book Parent/Teacher Resource Center
http://www.worldbook.com/ptrc/html/ptrc.htm

Teacher Forms

Homeschool Home
http://www.homeschoolhome.com/
TEACHER%20DESK%20page11.html

Science

Bill Nye the Science Guy Website
http://nyelabs.kcts.org/f_index.html

Cool Science for Curious Kids
http://www.hhmi.org/coolscience/

Discoveryschool.com
http://school.discovery.com/

Homeschooling Science Fun
http://www.suite101.com/welcome.cfm/
homeschooling_science_fun

NASA Quest
http://quest.arc.nasa.gov/home/index.html

The Frugal Homeschooler
http://www.suite101.com/welcome.cfm/
frugal_homeschooler

The Yuckiest Site on the Internet
http://yucky.kids.discovery.com/noflash/index.html

United States Environmental Protection Agency –
Explorer's Club
http://www.epa.gov/kids/

United States Environmental Protection Agency – Planet
Protector's Club
http://www.epa.gov/osw/kids.htm

Mathematics

Helping Your Child Learn Math
http://www.ed.gov/pubs/parents/Math/index.html

Knowledge Network Mathematics (K-12)
http://www.nhptv.org/kn/vs/mathla5.htm

Mathematics Lesson Plans (K-5)
http://www.col-ed.org/cur/math.html

Mathematics Links
http://www.geocities.com/Athens/Aegean/3446/mathematics.html

Mathematics Outline Structure
http://explorer.scrtec.org/explorer/explorer-db/browse/static/Mathematics/index.html

Mathematics Problem-Solving
http://www.rhlschool.com/mathv1-3.htm

Math-Tactics
http://www.leesummit.k12.mo.us/gwe/math/math.html

Geography/Social Studies

Geography Links
http://www.geocities.com/Athens/Aegean/3446/geography.html

Holiday Lesson Plans and Activities
http://members.aol.com/Donnpages/Holidays.html#FESTIVALS

Social Studies Resources
http://www.csun.edu/~vceed009/
socialstudies.html#Lesson

Art/Crafts

Crayola.com
http://www.crayola.com/

Home School Arts
http://www.homeschoolarts.com/

Lytyl Wytch Pagan Family Pages
http://www.lytlwytch.com/arts_&_crafts.shtml

OnePagan.com
http://www.onepagan.com/kids/

Pagan Parenting Page – Kids Stuff
http://www.paganparenting.net/kids/

Religion

The Internet Sacred Text Archive
http://www.sacred-texts.com/index.htm

Chapter Six
Integrating Spirituality

As pagans, our spirituality is usually an integral part of all that we are. It is not a separate subject to be studied out of context with the rest of our lives. It is a vital part of our daily lives, our annual cycles, and our very beings. Many of the pagan homeschoolers I have spoken with say that life and spirituality blend together as integral parts of one whole existence. These families live their lives in normal ways, including their children in their practices as they feel is appropriate.

One of my favorite aspects of home education is the fact that learning is not compartmentalized as it tends to become through modern, traditional schooling. This allows for spirituality to flow easily into everything that we learn and do. Through this type of education, our every action may be seen as a learning opportunity and a sacred act. We feel the guidance of our Gods and spirit guides as a tangible thing, and we know They are with us each step of the way.

Pagan children who are homeschooled often possess a strong sense of Self and a deep connection to

Spirit. Their interactions with a variety of people and situations teach them to live effectively and responsibly in the world--and often to try to make their world a better place. These are children who are respected by their home-educated peers for their accomplishments. They are not ridiculed as geeks. They invent things, write stories, develop computer games, and start local recycling programs. They follow their hearts and their natural creativity as they integrate all they have learned into real life.

Pagan homeschooled children (and all those from a strong spiritual background) have an additional opportunity to learn the spirituality of their families as a valid part of real life. They learn about religion, social studies, geography, earth science, and much more through the integration of spirituality and schooling. They are often encouraged to explore other religions that interest them. As a result, these children do more than give lip service to a religion or blindly follow dogma. They live their spirituality from a place that is solid and centered. This frequently gives them a stronger sense of Self and deeply held ethical standards.

Some families use the Wiccan Rede or the concept of cause and effect like Catholic families might use the Ten Commandments. These are ethical guidelines for how they live their lives. They are external manifestations of our respect for life and recognition that we are part of the cycles of life. If we hope to receive blessings, then that is what we put out there. It might be more accurate to say that spirituality is integrated into life itself, rather than simply into an educational context.

These are families who place a high value on respecting the natural world and all of life. Beyond religion, there is a subtle spirituality that pervades life and education. A great many families incorporate environmental awareness and ecological science with discussions on spirituality. This philosophy lends itself to spiritual and scientific learning and pagan homeschoolers take full advantage of this.

From my survey and other conversations, it appears that few families are actively teaching their children to be "pagan." Some are not sure how to go about that, but many simply live their own religion without any overt pressure on their children to choose or participate. Many make it a point to expose their children to a variety of spiritual paths until the children make this decision on their own. Several families were "mixed" with regard to religion and made it a point to expose their children to both belief systems.

Whether they actively teach their religion to their children or not, all of those responding to my survey said that they use the opportunities presented by their religious path to discuss their beliefs and answer any questions their children may have. They may use ritual elements, Moon phases, or festivals to instruct in various ways. Spirituality is often used by pagan homeschoolers to teach academic subjects. Not only does this allow us a wonderful way to integrate spirituality into general learning, but it also keeps it fun and interesting for everyone, providing a little extra motivation along the way.

One of the ways our son Karl learned to count and keep numbers straight even when they were out of order was through playing with his tarot deck. He learned to identify local plants and their uses through gathering sage for smudge sticks and accompanying me on herb walks. He is discovering music through learning to play a variety of drums and the Irish penny whistle. When we talk about history, politics and religion inevitably come up in the discussion. Each of these methods offers the opportunity to talk about spirituality and cultural beliefs. In my opinion, these are valuable lessons for all children who are being guided truly to think for themselves.

Children who are home educated in pagan families frequently have an in-depth grounding in comparative religions and the history of religion by the time they reach high school. It is true that many of these religions are not mainstream ones. However, these children learn to compare religions and understand how religions develop. They understand the role that governments, wars, and politics play in organized religion, and they learn to recognize the similarities and differences in various religions. They often gain an awareness of the common roots and spread of many religions.

In this chapter, I will explore a few of the many ways to use religion as a teaching tool and to incorporate academics into a living spiritual culture. As I explain throughout this book, these are intended to be a place to start. They are ideas and outlines that I hope will spark your own creative abilities in developing interesting educational experiences that incorporate a spiritual lifestyle. Only through returning to a more sacred way of living can we create a better world for future generations.

The Starry Heavens

Through a study of astronomy, we can learn about a surprising variety of subjects. Below I offer a few examples to serve as a guide while you develop your lesson plans. Similar studies can be done on the Sun, each of the planets in our solar system, and all known objects in the universe.

Phases of the Moon

Even before your child is ready to perceive the Moon as our only natural satellite or comprehend the differences in its composition and atmosphere from those of the Earth, the phases of the Moon will be apparent. The fact that its appearance changes is obvious once a child notices the Moon. This is particularly true if your family participates in some type of lunar phase obser-vance, like a drumming circle or ritual.

While a relative few families actually participate in a daily spiritual practice, many do observe the lunar cycles in a spiritual way. More of these families cel-ebrate the Full Moon than the New Moon or Dark Moon, but many pagan home educators honor most phases, at least during a study of the Moon.

Almanacs and astrological calendars will list the exact dates and times of the Moon phases, as well as the transits of other planets. The choice of whether or not to celebrate the cycles is clearly up to you. However, few traditions today hold to a rigid schedule of exact times. Most of us work when we are best able to. Even if pagan parents perform their own observances separate from their children, family celebrations revolve around the schedules of the family. For example, if the Moon is full at 2am on a Wednesday night, chances are good that the family will hold their celebration early in the evening on Tuesday or Wednesday.

Some families believe that the energy of the Full Moon, and some say the new and dark, lasts for three days before and three days after the phase is reached. Others believe it lasts for a total of three days: one day before, the day of, and one day after. Still others believe the working should only be done within twelve to twenty-four hours of the exact phase time and that the time leading up to the phase is most powerful.

Whatever you believe regarding the timing of Moon workings, the truth is that most family rituals do not involve much magick or serious spellwork. These are largely celebrations and opportunities for teaching. However, we can begin to teach our children about the energies associated with the phases at these times through discussion or simple magicks.

In general, the New Moon is the time for new beginnings, personal growth, and healing. During the waxing phase, we possess renewed strength and creativity. This is the time to integrate wisdom gained during the Dark Moon into our lives. At the Full Moon, things tend to come to a head. This is the energy of heightening sexuality, psychic influences, emotions, and protection. It is also a time of outward contact and connections, which may be why so many people come together on the Full Moon.

The waning phase is a time of completion, laying ground for next cycle, releasing, banishing, and healing. For some people, this is a time of higher psychic influences and abilities, often used for divination. And finally the Dark Moon is a period of renewal, often lower personal energy. Many of us use this time for going within and taking advantage of the energies of high intuition that frequently accompany this phase.

This is a good time to talk about the influence of the Moon in our lives and on our bodies. Through the use of a Moon journal or personal calendar, children can record feelings, events, dreams and anything else they feel is important. Over time, it will become apparent how the energies of each phase affect individual children and how they might best work with these energies in their own lives.

A study of the Moon often lends itself so well to feminine mysteries that boys may feel left out or wonder where they fit in all of this. It is important for them to be aware of the effects of the Moon and other planets on them as well and to recognize that the Goddess is within all of us. It might be helpful to offer some books that are specific to male spirituality at this time or during a study of the Sun. A few of the classics or more pagan-appropriate books are listed in the resources section at the end of this chapter.

Blood Mysteries

Parents of daughters should be encouraged to incorporate the Blood Mysteries into their studies. This is an ideal accompaniment to a Moon unit or a history unit. In ancient times, menstrual blood held power and honor. It is important for our young women to reclaim that power in their search for wholeness. I include a menarche[12] ritual in the chapter on Magick and Ritual.

It should be noted that many women no longer menstruate with Moon cycles. This is often due to artificial lighting, additives in food, and controlled environments. For us, the phases are personal as well as lunar. One's personal New "moon" would be the end of menstruation. At that time, we would embody the energies of the New Moon. While one's personal Moon is waxing, we prepare to ovulate. This is also the girl before menarche.

During a personal Full Moon, we are ovulating. We embody an adult woman in her full power and the Mother Goddess as we have the choice of whether or not to conceive. When our "moon" wanes, we ready for the release of our blood. This is also the time of the Crone and menopause. Young women may gain a greater sense of self-knowledge and control over life experience if they are encouraged to be aware of these personal phases.

For years, I attempted to do the usual group Full Moon celebrations. I was part of a women's circle for over one year and organized several children's Moon circles. None of this ever felt right to me. All I wanted to do was withdraw to my personal Moon Lodge or drum.

This is because my personal "moon" cycle does not correspond to that of the Moon. I menstruate on the Full Moon, not the Dark. In my personal cycle, this is my time for going within and calling for vision. My attempts at outward contact only resulted in irritation for me until I chose to work with my own cycles. Not only am I much happier now, my magickal workings are much more effective and productive.

It is possible to alter menstrual cycles through attuning oneself to the Moon and ensuring exposure to the light of the Moon during its cycle, particularly while you sleep. I have been quite successful in altering my cycles, but unless I continue to work at it, my phases return to my own personal normal. Rather waste energy forcing my cycle to align with the lunar ones, I simply work with my personal energy flow.

All children can attune to the Moon for this type of study through more than magick and ritual. There are some wonderful stories from cultures around the world that relate lunar folklore. Making up stories is an excellent exercise that allows personal creativity to flow through and develop. Families can also sample ethnic foods that have historically been associated with the Moon.

Few of the children I know like Oriental or Indian Moon cakes. Bean paste just doesn't seem to be a favorite among most American children. However, just about any cake, muffin, or bread can be baked into a Moon shape for lunar phase celebrations. This also provides an opportunity to incorporate kitchen safety, kitchen magick, and mathematics through measurement and time. Try this recipe for Moon Goddess cakes. It can be used as is or altered to fit your needs.

Saffron Crescent Cakes for Ashtoreth[13]

These are traditionally baked in honor of Ashtoreth, but they are appropriate for any Goddess who is associated with the Moon. Saffron is expensive, so you may prefer to substitute yellow food coloring, an additional 1/4 cup honey, or 1/2 cup chopped nuts instead.

You will need:

- 1 egg
- 2 cups all-purpose flour
- 3/4 cup milk
- 3 tsp baking
- 1/3 cup vegetable oil
- 1/2 tsp salt
- 1/4 cup honey
- 1/4 - 1/2 tsp saffron

Mix egg, milk, oil, and honey in a large bowl.
Add remaining ingredients and stir until just mixed.
Cut into wedges and roll up, starting at the rounded edge.
Place on greased cookie sheet with points down and shape into crescents.
Bake for 20 minutes at 400 degrees Fahrenheit.

To liven up a study of the Moon, it helps to engage all your senses, including the sense of humor. Any way you can bring action into the study is a good idea, especially for younger children. Flashlights are always fun to play with, and you may want to invest in a battery-charger to reduce battery-related cost and waste.

Using a ball or a round mirror as the Moon and a flashlight as the Sun, you can create an interactive tool for learning. Have your child pretend to be the Earth and hold the "Moon" out about a foot from their head. Hold the flashlight in a stationary position about head level for the child. Direct your child to stand in one spot, turn counterclockwise, and stop at each quarter turn. The reflection on the mirror or light on the ball will approximate the lunar phases, allowing the child a glimpse into the movements of Moon and Earth, relative to the Sun, that create the phases.

Read the facts below and consider what kind of story you can make up to explain some of them. Use these facts as the basis for mathematics exercises, especially with older children. Calculate how much farther away from us the Moon will be by your child's eighteenth birthday (see Fun Moon Facts). Ask your children to figure out how long ago the light you see actually hit the Moon if light travels at a speed of 300,000 kilometers per second. Ask them how the effects the Moon has on our Earth might also influence human physical bodies and emotions. Use the tide information as the starting point for a unit study on oceans.

Consider the effects of two or more moons, or no moon, on our planet and us. How might this affect the tides, growing seasons, and more? See if your library has a book with photos of the view of the Moon taken by astronauts. How would the view change from various points along the Earth's orbit or as a spaceship got closer to the Moon? The possibilities are only limited by our own creativity.

Fun Moon Facts

- The Moon is moving away from the Earth at a rate of about 4 centimeters each year.
- The Moon is mostly responsible for the Earth's tides.
- Because of the pull of the Sun, Earth, and Moon on each other, the Earth's rotation slows down about a millisecond each century.
- The Moon is egg-shaped. It is not a true circle.
- The Moon has "earth" quakes.
- The Moon produces no light of its own. It reflects the light of the Sun.

Astrology

While it is true that astrology is an involved discipline that even most adults have not mastered, it is most definitely not beyond the reach of the average child. In fact, I took my first astrology lesson at age eleven. While I did not obtain the depth of understanding that my mother had until many years later, I did gain a broader understanding of the planets and their interactions within our galaxy.

Through the study of astrology, I learned about the functioning of the solar system and eclipses. I explored what was known about constellations and asteroids. My math skills were tested time and time again as I performed the manual calculations necessary to cast charts. My reading skills had to develop in order to read the various books on the subject. My writing skills improved with each note I took and every interpretation I recorded.

Like all of us, children respond best when learning about themselves or their loved ones. Astrology can be a fun game of discovery and investigation as we delve deeply into the psyches of our friends and families. When I was young, I loved funny interpretations and astrological cartoons. I love Kim Rogers-Gallagher's books. Great for any age, *Astrology for the Light Side of the Brain* is ideal for children. Her images make the planets memorable and make their energies and associations very clear.

Our son and I started our study of the solar system while he was still watching "Blues Clues" on television. There is a great song on one episode of that show to introduce children to the names of the planets. They offer a catchy tune and a short description of each planet. For example, Mars is described as being the red planet. Ms. Rogers-Gallagher describes Mars as "a warrior all done up in red, feet planted squarely in fighting stance, sword drawn and ready to go."[14]

This is wonderful material, and it helped make our studies a great success. Singing the song from "Blues Clues," we built a clay model of the solar system. Then when we studied Mars, we were red Ninja warriors until we looked at our astrological charts. Then both of us got to be five-star military generals[15] thanks to the fact that we both have Mars in Capricorn. We played chess this way since we obviously *had* to be opposing generals.

Astrology and its associated mythologies can accompany any study of the solar system. It may be beneficial to explore similar Deities in cultural myths other than the Greek and Roman to add depth to your understanding of each planet and its energies. We spent a few days to a few weeks on each individual planet the first time our son studied the solar system in any real depth. He learned about early astronomers throughout history. As he learned of the geological and astronomical science of each planet, he also learned their mythologies and astrological associations.

During this study, we looked at each planet we could find in the sky through binoculars or a telescope. We looked it up on the Internet to get a better look, and then we found that planet in the astrological charts of family members. We turned it into a game of exploration and spent a considerable amount of time kidding each other about the less-than-glamorous aspects of our planets and their signs. Rather than being a dry study, the play and involvement of family members made it something easily memorable and interesting enough for a continued interest.

Earth as Teacher

My mother often says that Nature is our religion. It is true that for us the natural world is of vital importance, as it is for a great many pagans. No matter what place the Earth holds in your tradition, it can be an invaluable source of education and spiritual connection for children.

Not only do children tend to have an innate resonance with the natural world, but also many of the tools we use as pagans are derived from the Earth and Her creatures. Crystals, herbs, sacred woods, and more are natural resources. As such, they are replete with opportunities for teaching.

For many of us, the first step is to guide our children into alignment with the natural world. This is appropriate for young children who are not yet ready to handle the intellectual studies of the natural sciences. For children of all ages, it provides healing, grounding, and centering.

Below is an exercise to attune to nature spirits. It is written for use with crystals, trees, etc. but can be altered for use with Deities, ancestors, and more. This is a wonderful way for children to develop a psychic relationship with the natural world and their spirit guides.

Nature Spirit Attunement Exercise[16]

Begin by having the children feel and inspect whatever it is they will be "entering" during the meditation. Then have them get comfortable either sitting or lying down. If possible, have them hold the object during meditation.

Count your children down from ten to one or guide them to enter a light trance in your usual way.

Guide them to see the object before him, big as a house or bigger. Have the children inspect the outside of the object. Teach them to be respectful. Instruct them to ask permission to enter the object. Tell them to trust whatever comes up for them and if permission is denied, try another object or wait until they are better prepared. It may be beneficial to have the children tell you what they experience as it occurs. You can either record this with a tape recorder or write it down so details are not lost. This is also a great way for the children to develop their own abilities to retain information obtained in Other realties.

If permission is granted, guide them to enter the object through a door in the side of the object. Ask them what they see inside. Ask what the temperature is, the light level, how the walls feel. Ask if there are any sounds or smells that they are aware of. Get all of their senses involved in the experience.

Next, have them explore the object, giving you a narrative as they move along. Ask them if they encounter any beings within the object.

When they have explored most of the object or seem ready to come out, guide them back to the door they entered. Have them stop before leaving and give thanks to anyone or anything they encountered. Instruct them to ask if there are any last messages for them before they return to everyday reality. Give them some time to receive these.

Guide them back out through the door. As they leave, have them stop at the door and, taking a last look at the object, instruct them to leave an offering and thank the spirit of the object for this experience.

Count them back up from one to ten as usual, or in the same format you counted them down.

From this point on, any study of natural objects will be accompanied by a deep recognition of the life and sanctity of these objects. This awareness may be brought into studies of geology, natural history, plant biology, and more. Certainly these fields need to be simplified for younger children, but if you are willing to give them a chance and not wait to introduce these concepts, you might be surprised at how much they comprehend.

Children are naturally curious about the world around them. An early introduction of basic biology, migration, and ecology to interested children paves the way for an easier understanding of advanced concepts at older ages. At the age of four, our son explained the concept of "species" and the basic differences between mammals, birds, and reptiles to his grandmother. It was not a question of being advanced in this area nor was it something I planned. He was simply introduced to these concepts at a very early age through my work as a biologist and found them interesting. Through my willingness to follow his interests in this area, his understanding of the natural sciences grows each day.

Cloud Gazing

Divination and the development of psychic abilities can serve a myriad of purposes for both adults and children. When we are able to release our beliefs about the complexity of these tools and how they should be used, we can offer our children an early introduction and the confidence to experiment. In the process, we boost their self-esteem and faith in their abilities. We provide them with the tools they need to develop their own personal relationship with All That Is. Even more, we create a powerful forum for us to get to know each other better through play and sharing.

While divination and ritual are discussed in detail in chapter nine, there is a type of divination sometimes known as augury that rightfully belongs here. In many shamanic cultures, objects from nature are used for divination. These are traditionally found in the flight of birds or movements of other animals and the use of rocks, trees and cloud formations.

Children can have great fun lying on the grass and staring at the clouds overhead, especially when other people play along with them. For some of us, clouds are a rarity, and we spend plenty of time gazing at them when they do grace our desert skies. Clouds can be a wonderful canvas for scrying and other forms of divination.

This technique may also be used for rocks, tree bark, Water surfaces, and when gazing into a canopy of trees. To be honest, I've even used it to great success when staring at stucco ceilings. The idea is that we will project what we need or want to see on the random canvas before us. What we recognize or interpret gives us clues to the answers we need.

Before gazing into the clouds, close your eyes and take a deep breath, centering yourself into the Earth and Sky. Form a clear question and hold that intent until you feel it fill your being. As you open your eyes, blow the question out into the universe with your breath.

Then pick out three to five images that come immediately to mind when gazing at the clouds above and write them down with as much detail as you can. If you can hold the intent longer without your mind wandering, feel free to pick out more images. If you are guiding a young child who has not yet learned to write, write these images down for them.

When you are done cloud gazing, create an association web for each image. In an association web, start with one word, in this case the image you saw. From that word you draw lines connecting it with other words that are evoked by the main word. Some of these may spur additional smaller webs and all of this can bring up unconscious associations and answers. This exercise is a wonderful accompaniment or starting place for a study of clouds, the Water cycle, and weather systems.

Herb Lore

Most pagans use herbs in some form, whether in teas or through the use of incense. Many of us delve more deeply into this field by learning to create magickal oils, medicines, and other herbal products. The study of herbs can lead a child into plant ecology, biology, mathematics, magick, and basic first-aid. It is also a powerful tool for increasing self-confidence and an awareness of the interactions between body and mind.

I prefer to focus on one or two herbs at a time, learning them in real depth before moving on to others. This method has worked well for our son, but some children have an innate ability to remember the various plants and their uses. One way to help children gain a personal knowledge of the herb you are studying is to start a plant from seed. This enables the child to learn each life stage of the herb and the seasonal changes it may exhibit. It will also provide herbs to work with as the plant grows.

When children observe how adults work with

herbs they come to understand the variety of uses for common herbs. You may use rosemary to cook with on occasion. You may also use it as an incense for purification or in love and healing spells. As you cook with herbs, explain the other uses of the herbs to your children. Sharing stories that may go along with these explanations will help them remember.

Incorporating herbology into your homeschool arts and crafts will help bring the magick of life into education. It will also reinforce your teachings and help the children retain what they have learned. If you decide to make candles, consider making them herbal candles and bless them with a specific intent. You can add herbs to clay sculptures and even homemade paper (see chapter eight).

History through Mythology

Aside from ancient games and real-life stories, mythology is probably the best way to bring history alive for children. Myths and stories have a life to them that simple dates and names do not. Mythology not only gives us insight into the beliefs and practices of the people, but it also provides a view into how they perceived the world.

Several of the pagan home educators I know incorporate a great deal of mythology into their studies of ancient cultures. Other families will teach the evolution of cultures and politics through an exploration of changing myths and Deity names. This is an intriguing method because it also leads to the development of critical thought regarding politics and religion throughout the world and into modern times. Politics and religion are quite often closely related, and an understanding of one offers surprising insights into the other.

As is true with all other subjects, this is one that grows in complexity as your children grow up and learn more. When our son was five years old, he understood the different Deities and myths that are associated with a few regions of the world. He knew that we don't always share the same beliefs and practices that people long ago did. He had a basic understanding of the reasons an invading or changing culture would want to change the name of a Deity and later its rituals to better resonate with their people or their governmental policies.

But he didn't quite understand how invaders could actually change an honored Deity into a devil or a Goddess into a God. He thought of his special Deities and knew that They have been honored for thousands of years. He couldn't imagine Them ever disappearing from the memory of the people. While he understood why some people would try to affect such a change, he had difficulty believing that it could be successful. Now that he is older, that is beginning to change.

On the other hand, my friend's ten year old grasps this concept quite well and can tell you a few cultures where this has happened. He informs us that it happens over time for a variety of reasons. He is beginning to see the influence of more than simple violence on cultural change. He is starting to see the political influences as well.

Some educational philosophies stress the use of folklore, myth, and other stories in the education of young children. This is really an excellent way to begin at any age. If your children are older but have not been exposed to this type of learning, allow them to get involved in the wonderful stories first. Once their imagination and interest is involved, then you can guide them to look deeper into the myths of one culture and compare them to those of surrounding cultures.

Through myth, we can track the migrations of certain peoples. Some scholars believe that the Celts originated in India for reasons other than language. They point to the similarities between myths and Deity forms as evidence that the druids were a carryover of the educated priesthood caste among the Hindu culture. Not all agree with this interpretation, but it is a reasonable basis for creating hypotheses. The development and testing of hypotheses is an important element in education, particularly for the older child.

It has become clear that as migrating cultures moved in to new areas they often assimilated the Deities of the resident cultures. The names would change slightly to drastically, but many of the attributes and even some of the rituals retained the flavor of the previous Deity form. We see it from the Greeks and Romans and even among the Oriental cultures. Several native North American nations show similar evidence as the result of trading, intermarriage, or migration. It can be found among the Nordic and Icelandic peoples as well.

How you study mythology will depend on the ages and preferences of your children. Early on, these can be wonderful stories to read to young children. You might want to focus on a culture that attracts you or perhaps is a part of your ethnic heritage before moving on to comparative mythologies.

When Karl was six, we made a study of creation myths from around the world. We found a book with wonderful pictures and stories from every continent. As we went through the book, Karl created his own myths. We put these together on construction paper and bound them. In the process of creating Karl's Earth Book, Karl's Star Book, and Karl's Creation of the Solar System Book, he gained a personal understanding of how early peoples conceived of their myths. He learned to appreciate the human need to understand our world and began to formulate his own hypotheses. He also got practice writing, drawing, and problem solving.

Once children begin to use imagination in play, they often like to role play and dress up. This is a good age to introduce costuming and theatre to them. Costumes need not be elaborate. Our first knight's helmet was made of an old dog bone box and aluminum foil. But to Karl, it was a real knight's helmet. With it on, he was a great knight in search of adventure and protecting those in need. This was the beginning of a long-term fascination with Arthurian myth that led him to explore ancient Celtic games, the Crusades, weaponry, Arthurian tarot decks, and a huge variety of movies.

Plays may not interest all children. Those who do have an interest in theatre can act out their favorite myths, bringing them even more alive. A few children can become a complete stage crew, creating everything from the story, costumes, set design and more in the process. This can be the basis for a fantastic unit study.

Other children may not get excited about putting on plays, but they may respond to ritual. They may be more comfortable dressing as a favorite mythological character or Deity in ritual. They might prefer to learn enough about one being to invoke that energy during family ritual, particularly if other family members are participating in a similar manner.

When we were studying the Vikings, we each decided to pick a Deity and invite that Being to share in a Norse ritual with us. This is part of our heritage, so we incorporated some family history and geography into the unit. Before performing the rite, we each had to learn some key points about the Deities. We drew pictures of Them and dressed up in whatever way we felt was most appropriate for the Deity we represented. We wrote a poem or a few words for an invocation as preparation. When we set up the ritual space, we were each responsible for bringing in symbols or colors for our particular Deity.

Then we held our ritual. The focus was simply getting acquainted and honoring these Deities. It was short and simple with no intense magick. Even so, we each came away with a deeper knowledge of these Beings and the rites and symbols associated with Them. Afterward we talked about how these Deities might look and act if They were to decide to incarnate today in America.

Sometimes a full-blown ritual is overdoing it or just doesn't feel right for whatever reason. We happened to study ancient China near the end of September, right around the Autumn Equinox. After reading the story of Chang Er (also Chang O) whose image is seen in the Harvest Moon, we made paper lanterns and Moon cakes. We went outside to watch the Moon rise and gave thanks for our blessings throughout the year. It was a spiritual experience, but it was not an elaborate ritual.

Mythology can be an invaluable addition to the study of history. When I was a child, I always liked history. However, it was not until fifth grade when it all made sense and really drew my interest. My teacher made it all come to life for me. Suddenly history was more than names, places, and dates on paper. It had color and taste and music. He told interesting and often funny stories of real people. We built models of historical sites and made foods of the times. We even held a historical costume contest that everyone participated in.

This is the kind of educational experience that gets our minds and spirits involved. Now, almost thirty years later, I still remember that class and the joy I derived from learning there. I wish that every class I took could have been so imaginative and energetic. This was a teacher who loved teaching and loved his subject. As parents, we don't get jaded by oversized classrooms and seeing children fall through the cracks. These are our beloved children, and we love teaching them.

One's spirituality can be incorporated into every aspect of life through how you perceive and act. Homeschooling allows spirituality to be even more integrated into the child's total educational experience. They don't need to come home and consider how their schooling fits with the rest of their lives. They live it each day. I hope that this chapter will help to spark your own creativity in using traditional educational or magickal subjects to broaden your children's life experience.

Resources

NASA Jet Propulsion Laboratory
Teacher Resource Outreach
4800 Oak Grove Drive
Mail Code CS–530
Pasadena, CA 91109
818-354–6916
http://www.jpl.nasa.gov/

Books

Bevan, Finn (1999) *Beneath the Earth: The Facts and The Fables.* Children's Press.

Bledsoe, Karen E. and Candyce Norvell. (1997) *365 Nature Crafts & Activities.* Publications International, Ltd.

Bly, Robert (1992) *Iron John: A Book About Men*, Vintage Books

Buckley, Thomas and Alma Gottlieb. (1988) *Blood Magic: The Anthropology of Menstruation.* University of California Press.

D'Aulaires, Ingri and Edgar Parin (1992) *Book of Greek Myths.* Picture Yearling.

Drew, A.J. (1998) *Wicca for Men: A Handbook for Male Pagans Seeking a Spiritual Path*, Carol Pub Group

Durrell, Gerald. (1992) *A Practical Guide for the Amateur Naturalist.* Alfred A. Knopf.

George, Demetra. (1986) *Asteroid Goddesses.* ACS Publications.

George, Demetra. (1992) *Mysteries of the Dark Moon: The Healing Power of the Dark Goddess.* Harper San Francisco.

Heron Wind, Linda (1995) *New Moon Rising.* Delphi Press.

Keen, Sam (1992) *Fire in the Belly: On Being a Man,* Bantam Doubleday Dell Pub

Knight, Chris. (1991) *Blood Relations: Menstruation and the Origins of Culture.* Yale University Press.

Lofthus, Myrna (1983) *A Spiritual Approach to Astrology.* CRCS Publications.

Madden, Kristin (2000) *Pagan Parenting.* Llewellyn

Millman, Dan (2000) *Way of the Peaceful Warrior,* 20th Anniversary Edition,
H J Kramer

Moore, Robert L. and Douglas Gillette contrib., (1991) *King, Warrior, Magician, Lover: Rediscovering the Archetypes of the Mature Masculine,* Harper San Francisco

Moroney, Lynn. (1995) *Moontellers: Myths of the Moon from around the world.*

Morrison, Dorothy (2001) *Bud, Blossom, and Leaf.* Llewellyn.

Owen, Lara (1993) *Her Blood is Gold: Celebrating the Power of Menstruation.* Harper SanFrancisco.

Randall, Ronnie (2001) *A Children's Book of Myths and Legends.* Barnes & Noble Books

Rogers-Gallagher, Kim (1995). *Astrology for the Light Side of the Brain.* ACS Publications.

Star, Gloria (1988) *Optimum Child: Developing Your Child's Fullest Potential Through Astrology.* Llewellyn

Whitney, Charles A. (1989) *Whitney's Star Finder.* Alfred A. Knopf.

Zorn, Steven (1989) *Start Exploring Bullfinch's Mythology.* Running Press.

Magazines

Green Teacher
P.O. Box 1431
Lewiston, NY 14092
416-960-1244
greentea@web.net

In Canada:
95 Robert Street
Toronto, Ontario M5S 2K5

Ranger Rick
P.O. Box 2038
Harlan, IA 51593-0236
800-611-1599

Scientific American Explorations
P.O. Box 2053
Harlan, IA 51593-0236
http://www.explorations.org

Web Sites

Astro for kids: planets of our solar system
http://www.astronomy.com/content/static/
AstroForKids/default.asp

Menstruation.com
http://www.menstruation.com.au/sitemap.html

"Menstruation or, who says women can't stand the sight of blood?" by Alana Wingfoot
http://www.io.com/~wwwomen/menstruation/
index.html

Moon Phases
www.astro.wisc.edu/~dolan/java/MoonPhase.html

Moon Phases by Mama Witch
http://www.musicfortheGoddess.com/parent/sun_moon/moons.html

National Space Science Data Center
http://nssdc.gsfc.nasa.gov/planetary/planets/moonpage.html

NASA Lesson Plans
http://questdb.arc.nasa.gov/lesson_search.htm

Spacelink - Living in space
http://spacelink.nasa.gov/Instructional.Materials/NASA.Educational.Products/Living.In.Space/

Students for the Exploration and Development of Space (SEDS) presents The Nine Planets: A Multimedia Tour of the Solar System
http://www.seds.org

Witches' Voice - Moon Phases
http://www.witchvox.com/basics/luna.html

Chapter Seven
Learning with the Elements

A study of the elements and their associated directions can provide a treasure trove of information. What is more, like the festivals and mythology, the available information is so varied and extensive that this study can take a student from kindergarten all the way through college without becoming boring or redundant.

Neopagans generally work with at least four elements that are usually assigned to one of the cardinal directions. Many traditions also include Spirit as a fifth element. The elements and their associations are highly variable based on the specific neopagan or family tradition that is used.

The elements used in a pagan tradition are seen as symbols embodying magickal forces or qualities of energy. As children learn the path of their family, it is important that they recognize this and understand how to utilize each specific quality of energy. These qualities are sometimes linked to elementals, which are entities that reside in and hold the energy of the element. The elementals are also highly variable and, unless you follow a strict tradition that dictates the entities you work with, you might consider allowing your children to explore these entities through their studies and find those that resonate best with each child.

Many pagans link the directions and elements with the cycles of life and the seasonal changes. All things are placed on the Wheel of Life thereby aiding us in recognizing the cyclical nature of existence. This is a beneficial perspective for all of us, but it can be particularly useful to the older child or pre-teen for whom life has suddenly become intensely serious. Heartbreak and disappointment are a part of life and only time may ease the immediate pain, but knowing that happiness will cycle back to us may help.

In this section, I outline study suggestions for the five elements most commonly used by modern neopagans. Variations on this study might include a look at how other cultures perceive the "elements." Your children might be interested in investigating the Celtic Realms of Sea, Sky, and Earth or the Chinese elements and their place in the practice of feng shui.

Air

For most of us, Air is the intellect, inspiration, and dreams. Air is often placed in the East with the dawn and assigned the color yellow. Hawks and other birds are associated with Air. Related magickal tools are athames, swords or wands, and incense or smudge, depending on your tradition. Wind instruments also connect us with the powers of this element.

Air elementals are usually sylphs. Beings such

as fairies and angels may be found here as well. On the Wheel of Life, the East and Air are linked with infancy and young childhood. This is the dawn and early morning, the return of life after winter, and the spring.

Because this is the element of the mind, memory, and creativity, it is one that your older children may call upon for assistance as they move into more complex studies. When I was in school, I worked with Air any time I was faced with a difficult subject or during tests when I knew the answer but just could not retrieve it. Today, I work with all the elements regularly but call upon Air especially when I need help writing or coming up with new ideas.

Like all the elements, Air can be a study in itself or it can be a subtle backdrop to other studies through maintaining an awareness of that quality of energy that permeates learning, inspiration, and creativity of all forms. Air can serve as the vehicle for spells or meditations to assist the learning process. It is the energy associated with telepathy and often divination.

Breathing is probably the most personal and obvious use of Air. Without clean Air, we could not survive. An exploration of the Air element may include a study of Air pollution and trees or other plants. This is an ideal way to begin discussing oxygen and other atmospheric elements in the Periodic Table of Elements.

As I wrote earlier, an awareness of the breath can have wide-ranging benefits. It affects our well being: physically, emotionally, mentally, and spiritually. The breath can be used to excite or calm. The conscious alteration of inhalation and exhalation can induce trance, diminish pain, and remove blocks to creativity.

Teaching children to breathe deeply from the diaphragm gives them the tools to attain a greater degree of control over their own life experience. Observation of the breath can provide insight into one's emotional state. When we are afraid, stressed, or in pain, our breathing tends to become shallow and centered in the chest. When we are calm and balanced, breathing comes from deep in the belly and is much slower.

Divine Inspiration

To inspire means to inhale. It also means to excite or motivate. Furthermore, it means refers to guidance from beyond this world. We are each inspired in our own ways throughout life. Often the process of teaching and guiding our children can be tremendously inspirational, particularly when we see them using their own inspiration to create their lives.

Each child will manifest inspiration in a unique way, and we do them a great service when we encourage this. However, it is true that most children enjoy singing. Some may be more private about it, but music speaks to us all. In many shamanic cultures, shamans seek out or are gifted with a power song. This is not only a way to communicate with spirit allies, but it is a means of evoking one's own power and creativity.

Seeking the power song can be beneficial for pagan children. This is something that is specific to them; something private between them and their Gods or spirit guides. It allows them a feeling of personal power and authority. It is also something that they may call upon anytime they are feeling uncomfortable, frightened, or in need of an extra boost mentally, physically, emotionally, or spiritually. You may find that budding songwriters and singers blossom through this process.

Seeking the Power Song

Have them start very simply, by humming or intoning *Om*, either when they are alone or with you. Guide them to feel the vibration throughout their head and body.

Next use simple chants. This may be a combination of sounds or you may encourage them to repeat the names of spirit guides and their own name. Guide them to trust what comes up and sing it.

When they feel comfortable with this, encourage them to create a song about themselves, their feelings, goals, and Deities or spirit guides. This may be as simple or complex as they like, provided it is meaningful and they can really feel it. Allow them space to sing it when they feel drawn to. The more they sing, the more it will resonate with them and the more powerful it will be for them.

With time, all they will need to do is whisper the song or even just bring the feeling of it to mind in order to benefit from its power. The song will probably change as they grow up, and they should revisit it through singing it or meditating on it periodically.

Weather

Since Air can be so elusive, weather systems may be the best means of introducing this element. Depending on the type of weather, the Water element is often naturally included and specific Water projects will be discussed later in this chapter. Until a child is comfortable with the concept of elements as energies, it may help to focus on the effects of Air as an aid to bringing this concept into practical reality. A study of weather can be a wonderful companion to the study of Air as a magickal element.

Anemometer

You will need:

- A large pot of sand or dirt
- Pencil with eraser on the end
- 2 drinking straws
- One pin
- 5 small drinking cups
- Tape

Punch four holes the diameter of the drinking straws at right angles to each other in one cup near the top. Place two opposite holes slightly higher than the other two. Punch another hole the size of the pencil in the bottom.

Push the pencil through the bottom, point first, until the eraser sits just below the lowest pair of side holes.

Insert the drinking straws into the side holes so an equal length of straw extends from all sides.

Tape the remaining four cups to the ends of the straws, ensuring that they all face the same direction.

Mark one of the cups with colored tape or marker.

Pin the straws where they cross to the tip of the pencil eraser.

Secure the top of the pencil in the pot of sand, deep enough so that it does not fall over.

Have older children count the number of times the marked cup passes them in thirty seconds. Divide that number by five and you will have the wind speed in miles per hour. Younger children can simply tell you when the wind is just a gentle breeze, is blowing steadily, or is very fast.

Ask your children how a gentle breeze feels as opposed to a strong gusty wind. Encourage them to become the wind and tell you how they felt, physically and emotionally, as they acted like breezes or hurricanes.

The Sense of Air

Air is an ideal aid when introducing the five physical senses to children, particularly the sense of smell. In the centering exercise at the end of this chapter, Air is used both in centering through smell and touch. Young and old seem to enjoy the mystery smell containers that can often be found at educational exhibits and children's museums. This can be a fun game of learning as you teach your younger children about the sense of smell. Teens or children who have gone beyond basic chemistry can use this to supplement a study of organic aromatic compounds.

Mystery Smells

You will need:

- Plastic containers and caps used for 35mm film
- Clean yogurt containers with lids (if the lids are see-through, cover or paint them)
- Aromatic substances, such as cloves, cinnamon, or mint

Fill each container with a different aromatic substance and label them on the bottom. You may prefer to poke a hole in each cap so the substance cannot be seen. Cover this with tape when not in use.

Go Fly A Kite

Kite flying is something that can be done just about anywhere, and it provides an easy method of connecting with Air energies. As homeschoolers, you may want to create your own kites for educational purposes. This allows for time working with art, math, geometry, aerodynamics, and construction methods as you experiment with various designs to find what works best.

Older children can develop vocabulary words such as lift, drag, and surface area through kite building. An in-depth examination of gravity can result from playing with kites. When studies progress into the higher sciences, children can use kites and paper or balsa wood airplanes as manipulatives for studying Bernoulli's Principle.

History and Social Studies can be included through an exploration of kite flying throughout the world. For example, the kite is believed to have originated in China over 3000 years ago. In Japan, kites are often created for very definite reasons. It is considered an honor to receive a kite as a gift in Japan, and this is a traditional New Year's gift for children. Benjamin Franklin, Alexander Graham Bell, Wilbur and Orville Wright, and Leonardo da Vinci all used kites to develop their theories and ideas.

Encourage children to come up with additional ways to work with kites. Air is a powerful vehicle for spells. See if children can create clever ways of using kites to launch their spells. You might find that using a kite in visualizations is just the thing to assist children in accessing inspiration and finding answers to their questions.

Gemini, Libra, and Aquarius are the astrological Air signs. Air signs relate to the intellect, the need to be social, ideas, and logic. We can study the influence of Air as magickal element by investigating how it manifests through the zodiacal Air signs. See if your children can find the Air signs in their own astrological charts. This can easily be combined with an astronomy or mythological unit study of the constellations and their stories.

Older children can choose a topic of study associated with Air and follow it in a way that best interests the individual child. One child may decide to investigate birds and learn about nesting behavior and migration. Another child may prefer to spend some time learning about and meditating on Deities associated with Air, such as Hermes or Mercury and Arianrhod or Athena.

Fire

No matter what direction the element of Fire is placed in, its energy is passionate, transformative, and unquestionably alive. Among neopagans, it is often found in the South with the noonday Sun and summer. Fire burns bright among our youth, and this is the time of life associated with the South.

The elementals and other beings which are commonly linked with Fire are the Jinn, the Phoenix, and elemental Salamanders, though some traditions relate Salamanders to Water. Animals which are often seen as Fiery or which may be placed in the South are coyote, reptiles, and the stag. The Wand is seen as a tool of Fire in many traditions, though some use the Sword in this place.

Fire spurs physical activity, and we can feel the spark within whenever we move. For the homeschooler, physical education does not often mean a set time of kickball and square dancing. Homeschoolers ice skate and do yoga. They take ballet, karate, and swimming lessons. They join others for African dance and hikes. Home-educated children are rarely couch potatoes. Quite the opposite, they get plenty of physical exercise without regimenting the fun out of it. The Fire of joy that free activity brings is maintained as we enjoy the physical and emotional benefits of it.

Because of its passionate and often sexual nature, Fire can be a difficult element to master, especially as children near puberty. However this nature also makes it an important element to integrate with balance. Handled well, Fire has the ability to purify one's being and transform simple desire into a truly Divine experience of illumination. Used with wisdom, Fire brings courage and strength along with truly inspired creativity and a great ability to succeed.

Flame Vision

Fire has been used for scrying throughout the world. Whether you gaze at a candle flame or peer deeply into a bonfire, this element can be called on to help you see at a distance, into the future, or within yourself. Fire is purifying and transformative as it sparks our intuition and innate creativity.

Scrying can be a tremendous benefit for children because it offers them a tool for gaining self-knowledge. With an ability to really know their own motivations, fears, strengths, and weaknesses, children develop a control over their own life experience that most of adults still strive toward. When they are uncomfortable or have a fight with someone, they have the tools available to uncover the reasons for their feelings and actions. They are also able to gain some insight into the reasons behind the conflict. Armed with knowledge, they can begin to work through their shadows and create life from a clearer state of being.

With so many societal blocks to trusting intuition and maintaining one's faith in spirit guides, the use of divinatory tools can boost a child's self-confidence and faith in the flow of energy through this world and others. With each success, their trust in their own intuition and abilities to find their own answers is supported. While having fun, they are encouraged to develop, rather than give up or block, their innate magickal abilities.

Young children should never use Fire without supervision. Even older children should be educated in Fire safety before being permitted to use Fire on their own. That said, we can move on to a discussion of scrying methods. Scrying can be a difficult technique to master. However, children tend to take to it more easily than most adults because of their active imaginations and relative lack of intuitive blocks. Use your own discretion in guiding younger children through Fire visioning. It may help to have them visualize the situation at hand, and you may want to record what they see for them so you can discuss it together when they have finished scrying.

To aid your psychic opening, you might choose to anoint the candle or your own Third Eye[17] with essential oil of jasmine, myrrh, or sandalwood. Alternately, you may prefer to count yourself down from ten to one into a relaxed state of being. Then light a new white candle. Allow the flickering of the flame to gently lull you into a light trance. Many people find the use of a simple chant aids the process greatly. Try chanting this three times:

> *Flame of Fire, Flame of Light,*
> *Bring me now the Second Sight.*
> *Bless me and help me see*
> *All that lies within me.*

Sit quietly and continue to gaze at the flame.

Rather than resisting the thoughts that may come up, acknowledge them without judgment and allow them to pass you by. If you are scrying for a specific purpose, hold that purpose in mind as you gaze. You may begin to see images in the flame or in your mind. Some of the thoughts that come up may be obviously related to your purpose or they may come up again and again, demanding a closer look.

In the beginning, it may seem like you are seeing nothing but stick with it. Practice will increase your ability to See, and you may begin to receive the answers you seek through dreams. With trust and practice, scrying will become as easy a tool for you to use as a tarot deck.

The Sun

The Sun is an obvious object of Fire. It also offers a wide range of educational opportunities. With some basic instruction in Sun safety, this can be a safe and versatile teaching tool. Like the Moon, the Sun draws children's attention. They notice the way it appears to rise and set. As they get older, they recognize that it always rises in the East and sets in the West. At some point, they may even realize that the exact location of sunrise and sunset vary with the season.

This is a good time to work with the male aspects of being, particularly if you have boys who were feeling left out during a Moon study. After all that talk about menstruation, they might like to consider the type of manhood ritual they would like to experience. What goals do they hold for themselves as men? Also encourage your daughters to develop an awareness of the God within.

Solar studies lead naturally into studies of the cardinal directions, particularly East and West. The Sun sparks discussion on day and night, the seasons, the movement of the Earth, and the rest of the solar system. This can include studies of solar energy, light, and even time. Sundials are simple to make and children of all ages can learn more about time from this type of project.

Sun Facts

- The Sun is the largest object in our solar system.
- 1.3 million Earths could fit inside the Sun.
- Solar energy is produced by nuclear reactions in the core of the Sun.
- The core temperature of the Sun is 27,000,000 degrees Fahrenheit. It is 11,000 degrees Fahrenheit at the surface and a mere 7000 degrees Fahrenheit in the dark area of sunspots.
- Scientists believe the Sun has been around for almost 5 billion years and will last for another 5 billion years before it becomes a red giant and consumes the Earth.
- Because the Sun is liquid, it does not all rotate on its axis at once. Surface rotation can take anywhere from twenty-five to thirty-six days.
- Solar flares are eruptions on the Sun that can disrupt communications and power grids on Earth.

Safe Sun Viewing

Most of us know that looking directly at the Sun can cause blindness. The use of binoculars or telescopes to view the Sun directly increases this risk dramatically. This is something children need to be taught.

Blindness is caused by the tremendous amount of light produced by the Sun, both visible and invisible. Even the best sunglasses cannot protect human eyes from the wide range of damaging light. The cardboard or Mylar viewers that are sometimes sold when an eclipse will be visible are also a cause for concern. These may not fit properly, scratches and even tiny holes will diminish their effectiveness, and not all are made to necessary specifications. However, there are methods of viewing the Sun that are safe.

A Pinhole Viewer

Projecting the image of the Sun is a popular method of safe viewing. A pinhole viewer is a common way to do this, and it has been around for decades. To make this viewer, all you need is one piece of plain cardboard, a white sheet of paper, and a pin. Punch a hole with the pin into the cardboard. Be sure not to make the hole too big.

Standing with your back to the Sun, hold the cardboard with the hole at your shoulder and the white paper at arm's length. On the paper, an upside-down image of the Sun will appear. The image can be altered by changing the distance between cardboard and paper. Never look through the pinhole directly at the Sun.

Aries, Leo, and Sagittarius are the astrological Fire signs. Fire signs relate to enthusiasm, activity, and spontaneity. We can study the influence of Fire as magickal element by investigating how it manifests through the zodiacal Fire signs, just as we did with the Air signs. See if your children can find the Fire signs in their own astrological charts.

Older children can study Fire in the way that best interests each individual. One child may decide to investigate the Summer Solstice through astronomy and legend. Another child may prefer to spend some time learning about the Deities associated with Fire, such as Ra or Vulcan and Brighid or Pele.

Water

Water is often found in the West in neopagan traditions. Its energy is emotional and intuitive. Water and the West are frequently associated with the sunset and autumn. On the Wheel of Life, this is the time of maturity.

The elementals and other beings which are commonly linked with Water are Undines, Merfolk, Sirens, and elemental Salamanders, though some traditions relate Salamanders to Fire. Animals which are often seen as Watery or which may be placed in the West are bears, fish, buffalo, frogs, and turtles. The cup, cauldron, and chalice are the tools of Water.

A study of the element of Water naturally coincides with a study of the Moon, the oceans, and the importance of Water to all of life. Many families choose to learn about Water pollution and Water conservation at this time. If you are studying chemistry, the Water molecule is one of the easiest to construct with some straightened-out paper clips and two different colors of clay.

Because of its emotional nature, Water can be an important element to explore. In modern society, it can be especially valuable for boys because of a pervading societal insistence that young men be stoic and unemotional. All of us can have difficulty identifying exactly what we are feeling and why at times. Children are still learning about emotion and how to handle it in their own lives. Working with Water can help.

Water Vision

Like Fire, Water can purify and stimulate our visioning abilities. In place of a candle flame, we may scry just as effectively using Water. Use your own discretion in guiding younger children through this process. It may help to have them visualize the situation at hand and you may want to record what they see for them so you can discuss it together when you have finished scrying. If you choose to use a chant, you might try something like this:

> *Water of Rain, Water of Sea,*
> *Bring the Second Sight to me.*
> *Bless me with your sacred flow.*
> *Help me understand what Water will show.*

Set aside a bowl to be used only for this purpose. It is preferable for each family member to have his or her own bowl for scrying. The interiors of scrying bowls are frequently black, but this is not necessary.

Fill the bowl at least halfway with Water. Pass first your left hand, then your right hand over the surface of the Water, aligning your energy with that of the Water. Ask that the spirit of the Water allow you to honestly and gently see yourself in the bowl. If there is a certain situation or emotion you need to deal with, ask for specific guidance in seeing this clearly.

Give yourself time to see whatever shows up. If you see only symbols, ask that they be made more clear, or give yourself additional time to allow the meanings to flow into your conscious mind. Know that you can focus on specific elements of the image by simply relaxing and allowing yourself to become more open. What you are looking at in this exercise is your own inner self and you control your access to it.

If you need guidance in making a decision or handling something differently in the future, ask for it. Your spirit guides and the spirit of the Water will hear you.

Ask if there is anything else you need to see at this time and give yourself time to experience whatever may come up.

When you are satisfied that the greatest benefit was achieved in this session, give thanks to the spirit of the Water and to yourself. Dispose of the Water with respect and thanks, either in a garden or as an offering to the spirits of your home.

Water Cycles

Water cycles throughout our planet just as do other

elements, energy, and nutrients. An investigation of the Water cycle can accompany a discussion of the Wheel of Life and the natural cycles of day and night, death and rebirth, and the seasons. The Water cycle is something that is readily accessible and a full year is not required to see it in action in our world or through experiments. This is also something that can be taught to a child as young as four or five.

It is best to begin with an introduction to the three states of Water: ice, liquid, and gas or vapor. Melting ice or freezing Water to show a child this transformation is a relatively simple thing. Showing them the change into gas or the condensation back to Water takes a bit more creativity. The exercise below will take you all the way through the Water cycle in your own kitchen.

Mini Water Cycle at Home

You will need:

- Stove
- Pot of Water
- Aluminum pie plate
- Ice

Heat the pot of Water on medium heat. Observe any changes in the Water as it heats

Place the ice in the pie plate and hold the plate above the pot of Water. Notice any changes in the ice. Hold the plate six to twelve inches above the Water for two or three minutes.

Look for droplets to form on the bottom of the

plate. Note how long it takes for them to begin to fall.

Water Music

Music is one thing that can truly speak to our souls. Good music bypasses the rational mind and impacts many of us directly at our hearts and through our physical bodies. This type of music falls within the realm of the Water element.

Using Water, we can make a variety of sounds that can create music, with a little practice. The first and most simple of these is to fill glasses with varying levels of Water and run a wet finger around the rim, like many people do with crystal wine glasses. You may also blow into soda bottles filled with various amounts of liquid. The creation of a Water drum is an exercise in itself.

Water Drums

The drum is often believed to speak in the rhythms of Mother Earth and is associated with the Earth element. It is often combined with Fire at drumming circles outside around bonfires. The Water drum adds the element of Water and all its associated energies to those of the drum.

Water amplifies sound and is therefore an interesting addition to a drum. Water drums are not common among neopagans, but they are known among some native North American and African peoples. Some of these cultures created their Water drums as hollow gourds or smaller bowls of various sizes placed within a larger vessel of Water. The gourds or bottom of the smaller bowls are then struck with a mallet to create the sound. This is a rather simple thing to create and is a wonderful project to do even with young children.

As children grow older, they tend to want more complex projects to work on. The creation of the other type of Water drum is perfect for the older child. It may be equally challenging for the parent and this adds a level of difficulty and enthusiasm for all concerned.

Creating the Water Drum

You will need:

- A deep bowl of waterproof clay or metal or a waterproof wooden box
- A goatskin head that will extend at least five inches beyond the rim of the opening
- A length of rope at least ten feet and preferably non-stretch
- Eight small stones

Soak the goatskin in Water until it is soft and pliable, about an hour.

Fill the bowl or box with Water about one-quarter to one-third full.

Stretch the skin over the opening and pull it tight.

String one loop of rope around the rim just tight enough to hold the skin in place.

Pull the slack out of the skin from beneath this rope loop.

Place the stones beneath the skin one by one,

stringing the rope around them to hold each in place tightly. The stones should be about halfway between the rim and the end of the skin.

Loop another length of rope around the rim, tying the stones into place more securely. Make one more loop before tying this off above one of the stones.

Now string the rope tightly around the bottom of the drum, looping it into the upper circles between each of the stones. Pull these strands very tightly and tie the rope off at the top circle.

Cancer, Scorpio, and Pisces are the astrological Water signs. Water signs relate to emotion, instinct, and perception. We can study the influence of Water as magickal element by investigating how it manifests through the zodiacal Water signs, just as we did with Air and Fire signs.

Children may prefer to study Water in their own ways. One child may decide to investigate the Water cycle or wetland ecosystems. Another child may prefer to spend some time learning about the Deities associated with Water, such as Manannan or Poseidon and Yemaya or Cerridwen of the Cauldron.

Earth

Neopagan traditions frequently place Earth in the North with winter and night. Its energy is practical and dependable. On the Wheel of Life, this is the time of elderhood and the transition of death and rebirth.

The elementals and other beings which are commonly linked with Earth are Gnomes, Dwarfs, and all the Little People in cultures around the world. Animals which are often associated with Earth or which may be placed in the North are horses, burrowing animals, and snakes. Many people place turtles here. Pentacles and crystals or other stones are the tools of Earth.

A study of the element of Earth is a perfect accompaniment to a study of ecosystems, animals, and geology. Many families choose to learn about recycling and habitat conservation at this time. The study of money and mathematics fall within the realm of Earth. Other related interests include paleontology, archeology, and the use of stones and plants in healing.

Because of its grounding nature, Earth can be exceptionally valuable, especially for children with an abundance of Air, Fire, or Water in their astrological charts. All of us need Earth when we are upset, stressed, and need to ground out excess energy. When we are feeling alone or disconnected, Earth can fill that empty place and remind us that we are never alone as long as we remain open to the energy of the Earth.

Anatomy and Energetics

The physical body is our Earthly residence as long as we choose to be incarnate on this planet. Anatomy and physiology are common subjects in compulsory schools and basic anatomy is something everyone should know. As pagan home educators, we may take this to another level.

We recognize that there is much more to us than the physical body. We also understand that our energy systems are intimately related to the functioning of our physical bodies. Therefore, an exploration of anatomy in a pagan household is bound to be very different than the explorations of schools or laboratories. Older children may want to take this further into a study of subtle energy or quantum physics.

We may begin by looking at the seven chakras associated with the physical body. The colors and even specific locations of these may vary according to your tradition, but the general concept is the same. Each of the "physical" chakras relates to an area of the physical body, an emotional or mental state, a color, and various stones.

General Associations
of the Seven Major Physical Chakras

Chakra	Associations
1-Root	spinal column, kidneys survival, physical sensation, passion red and black black tourmaline, onyx, garnet, bloodstone
2-Abdomen	reproductive and lymphatic systems sexuality, ambition orange carnelian, amber

3-Solar Plexus stomach, liver, adrenals
will, manifestation, intuition, intellect
yellow
citrine, tiger eye

4-Heart   circulatory system, thymus
emotions, love, healing, nurturing
green or pink
malachite, emerald, rose quartz, rhodo-
chrosite

5-Throat   lungs, throat, thyroid gland
communication, creativity
blue
aquamarine, turquoise

6-Third Eye   ears, eyes, nose, pineal gland, lower
brain, inspiration, psychic sensitivity
dark blue/indigo
lapis lazuli, sodalite

7-Crown   pituitary gland, upper brain
out of body travel
direct Otherworldly experience
violet
amethyst, fluorite

After investigating the chakras, you might move on to look at the energy bodies or auric levels that are associated with the individual chakras. Direct experience is preferable in any study but particularly when investigating metaphysical or magickal topics. Any number of learning games can be devised around the human energy field.

Stones of the Chakras

An ideal first rock collection can be comprised of stones associated with the chakras. If possible, collect one stone for each chakra. These need not be those listed above. They may be others of the same color range. You may also use clear quartz in place of specific stones and charge the quartz with the required color energies.

Choose one stone per week and learn all you can about it. Use the Nature Spirit Attunement exercise in chapter six to develop a working relationship with each individual stone. Practice aligning the chakras by placing the correct stone on each chakra and taking note of how this makes you feel physically, mentally, and emotionally. Encourage your children to draw the stone or write a story about it. Older children may be guided to investigate the origins of the stone: whether it is metamorphic, igneous, or sedimentary; where in the world these stones are found; and how they are mined.

Trees

Trees have been revered by cultures throughout the world. These are the Standing People, the physical manifestations of dryads, and the material used to make drums and other sacred objects. They are homes and grocery stores for a multitude of wild creatures. Trees provide us with clean Air, shelter, fuel, and much more.

For the pagan child, trees are friends and sacred beings. They offer comfort and guidance in times of need. Many of us find that our entire perspective changes once we spend time among the trees. The Tree People teach us patience and to stand firm yet flexible. They also remind us that all of life goes through cyclical changes.

A Tree Friend

Developing a personal relationship with a tree is the first step to connecting with that energy and gaining guidance from these special beings. Some children innately bond to a tree in their yard or neighborhood, particularly if their families support this. Many pagan parents or adults who were raised pagan have fond memories of a special tree that became a dear friend as they were growing up.

Developing this relationship is similar to the ways in which we develop other relationships. Ideally children should choose a tree that attracts them in some way. Have them begin by spending time with their tree at least once every two weeks. Encourage them to really get to know the tree. See if they can identify the species and help them learn more about that type of tree. Write down or draw the seasonal changes this tree goes through. Observe any other creatures which use this tree in some way.

You might suggest that your children take a thin piece of paper and a crayon or chalk and make a rubbing of the tree's bark to hang up in their rooms. If they find acorns, pinecones, or small branches lying on the ground beneath the tree, encourage them to bring one home. This would be a nice addition to a child's personal altar and assist that child in aligning his or her energy with that of the tree. Use the Nature Spirit Attunement Exercise in chapter six to help them get to know the tree on a deeper level.

There are an almost unlimited amount of studies that can accompany the process of getting to know a tree or trees. Children can study the Celtic *ogham* script. They might look at logging practices and their effects on old-growth forest or certain animal species. You could begin a unit study of the ancient and sacred uses of various woods in your area or throughout the world. Your children might also prefer to ask their new tree friend for guidance in deciding what to study next.

Taurus, Virgo, and Capricorn are the astrological Earth signs. Earth signs relate to practicality, dependability, and the physical world. We can study the influence of Earth as magickal element by investigating how it manifests through the zodiacal Earth signs, just as we did with the other elements.

Older children can follow their interests in studying Earth. One child may decide to investigate how oil was created or the financial structure that has grown up around this resource. Another child may prefer to spend some time learning about the Deities associated with Earth, such as Cernunnos or Pan and Gaia or Epona.

Spirit

Spirit is that which permeates all things. It connects us to each other, to the Gods, and to other inter-dimensional beings. You can incorporate Spirit in home education simply through how you interact with each other and the sacred. As parents, you can make time for meditation during the day. You can also encourage the use of journals, music, or artwork. Each form of creativity allows a direct experience of Spirit and a personal interpretation of how Spirit manifests.

Dreaming and other Pathworkings

We are all born with an innate ability to dream and journey. In fact, lucid dreaming is really just journeying (or astral travelling) while the physical body sleeps. Since we enter the physical form from the Otherworlds at birth, we retain those abilities and that connection to these Worlds until the influences of family or society create blocks in us. Young children tend to be very active on an astral level and have easy access to inspired imagination.

Parents can support and encourage these abilities simply through showing an active interest in them. When a child talks about dreams, we can listen attentively and ask questions. Through friendly questioning, we can encourage our children to retrieve more detail and begin to understand their own personal symbolism at an early age. Parents can also reciprocate by sharing any dreams they have with their children and answering their questions. Both parent and child can grow through this process.

As children develop their language and listening skills, and begin to engage in imaginative play, shamanic journeying and guided meditation can become valuable tools for them. Children don't often try to analyze what they experience. At the younger ages, they don't care whether or not they are making it up. They may well be making it up, but they are creating from honest inspiration. As a result, they can gain some truly surprising insights and answers through the use of these tools.

With a basic explanation of the Otherworlds, children can become masters of this type of out-of-body travel. They tend to respond well to the traditional descriptions of the Lowerworld as Earth-like, the Middleworld as this reality, and the Upperworld as celestial in nature. When we explain to them that time and space do not exist without the physical body, they are able to delve into the past and future while seeing what is happening at great distances.

When using guided meditation, it is best to keep things simple and short in the beginning. Long, complicated meditations are likely to only bore your children, including teens, and result in a need to release pent-up energy.

Exercise: Centering Through The Senses[18]

Sit or stand quietly in a place in nature where you feel safe and are unlikely to be disturbed. Take a deep breath and breathe out all your tensions, all your worries. Ask the Spirits of the Place for their permission before moving forward with the exercise. If you feel strongly that permission is not given, try another place or another time.

Focus on your sight. Allow your eyes to relax.

Rather than focusing on what you see, simply be with the process of seeing. Permit any thoughts that come up to pass through your mind and float away. Try not to categorize or label what you see. Enter into communion with its essence. Become aware of any changes in your sight as your body slows and centers. You may notice light and shadow more, or you may be increasingly aware of new colors around you.

Now, close your eyes and focus on your hearing. Don't strain to hear anything, just gently be with whatever you hear. Permit any thoughts that come up to pass through your mind and float away. Try not to categorize or label what you hear. Enter into communion with its essence. Become aware of any changes in your hearing as your body slows and centers. Feel yourself grounding and opening to the natural world.

Change your focus to your sense of smell. Don't actively sniff the Air, just gently observe whatever you smell. Permit any thoughts that come up to pass through your mind and float away. Try not to categorize or label what you smell. Enter into communion with its essence. Become aware of any changes in your sense of smell as your body slows and centers. Feel yourself grounding and opening to the natural world.

Now focus on your sense of touch. Feel the Earth beneath you, the Sun and wind on your skin, your clothes, and the feel of your body. Permit any thoughts that come up to pass through your mind and float away. Try not to categorize or label what you feel. Enter into communion with its essence. Become aware of any changes in how you feel as your body slows and centers. Feel yourself grounding and opening to the natural world.

Allow each of these senses to combine. Feel your entire body resonate with awareness. Permit any thoughts that come up to pass through your mind and float away. Try not to categorize or label what you feel. Enter into communion with All That Is. Become aware of any changes in how you feel as your body slows and centers. Feel yourself grounding and opening as you become One with the natural world.

Discuss personal boundaries with your children, particularly before and after performing this exercise. Be aware of any differences in how you define yourselves and your boundaries once you have completed the exercise. You might define yourself by your physical boundaries beforehand. You may include your religion as well or your nationality and ethnic heritage. After this exercise, many people find that the boundaries are blurred in a way. Suddenly the individual includes All That Is or feels a greater connection to the Spirit in the world around them.

While we focus on individual elements for specific energies, the goal for many of us is to achieve a balance of all the elements. We strive toward total integration of each element so that we may find that energy within when we are in need, rather than always having to look outside ourselves. The ritual below was written with the child in mind, but it is equally effective for an adult.

While the ritual below is a serious one, it is a ritual for children and should reflect that. Allow them some leeway in setting up one main altar and four directional altars. This can be an excellent way for children to utilize their creativity and really work with what they have learned about each element or direction

For example in a recent community ritual, we gave the children free rein over the directional altars. Our son made a Fire altar with a red chili pepper altar cloth, a toy Fire Pokemon, a stuffed dragon, two plastic Captain Planet Fire power rings, and a red glowstick. His friend and her mother created beautiful golden origami peace cranes for the East altar and made wire bubble wands for all the children to help them invoke Air.

Another family covered their North and Earth altar with stones, crystals, plants and dirt. The family responsible for the Water altar placed a goldfish in its bowl on the table and called in the element using Water squirting rings. The main altar was a combined effort by everyone present, adults and children alike. The children truly felt that this was their ritual by being such a vital part of it.

The ritual below is written using the most common neopagan directional associations for each element. Feel free to alter this to suit your particular path and your children's ages.

Ritual: Elements Within

If possible, perform this ritual outside. Set up one altar for each direction and one main altar. Have present on the directional altars: incense or smudge for Air, a glowstick or candle for Fire, a bowl of Water for Water, and a stone and seeds for Earth. Include symbols of your main spirit guides or Deities and something to represent you on the main altar.

Cast the circle or create sacred space in your preferred manner.

Consecrate this space with each of the elements by walking around the circle with each representative. Begin with the incense or smudge of Air. Then use the glowstick or candle flame for Fire. Move on to the Water from the bowl for Water. End with the seeds for Earth.

Facing East with arms outstretched: *I come to the East for inspiration and guidance of the mind. I thank you for your presence in my life and ask to receive the blessings of Air.*

Sit in the East and gaze into the smoke from the incense or smudge. Breathe deeply of the scent and meditate on how Air manifests in you. Consider your strengths and challenges in those things ruled by Air. Allow these meditations to flow into the incense or smudge. When you are ready, pick up the incense or smudge and, walking a clockwise spiral to the center, place it on the main altar.

As I place this incense/smudge at the center of my circle, I accept and integrate the Air within myself. I do this without judgment and with perfect love and perfect trust.

Facing South with arms outstretched: *I come to the South for purification and guidance of the spirit. I thank you for your presence in my life and ask to receive the blessings of Fire.*

Sit in the South and gaze into the glowstick or candle flame. Meditate on how Fire manifests in you. Consider your strengths and challenges in those things ruled by Fire. Allow these meditations to flow into the glowstick or candle. When you are ready, pick it up and, walking a clockwise spiral to the center, place it on the main altar.

As I place this glowstick/candle at the center of my circle, I accept and integrate the Fire within myself. I do this without judgment and with perfect love and perfect trust.

Facing West with arms outstretched: *I come to the West for comfort and guidance of the heart. I thank you for your presence in my life and ask to receive the blessings of Water.*

Sit in the West and gaze into the bowl of Water. Meditate on how Water manifests in you. Consider your strengths and challenges in those things ruled by Water. Allow these meditations to flow into the Water in the bowl. When you are ready, pick up the bowl and, walking a clockwise spiral to the center, place it on the main altar.

As I place this bowl of Water at the center of my circle, I accept and integrate the Water within myself. I do this without judgment and with perfect love and perfect trust.

Facing North with arms outstretched: *I come to the North for grounding and guidance of the body. I thank you for your presence in my life and ask to receive the blessings of Earth.*

Sit in the North, holding the stone and seeds, and meditate on how Earth manifests in you. Consider your strengths and challenges in those things ruled by Earth. Allow these meditations to flow into the stone and seeds. When you are ready, place the stone into the container of seeds and, walking a clockwise spiral to the center, place them on the main altar.

As I place this stone and seeds at the center of my circle, I accept and integrate the Earth within myself. I do this without judgment and with perfect love and perfect trust.

Standing at the main altar: *I honor the elements within me, and I give thanks for your blessings in this rite of self-knowing. May I be guided to continue the work of this rite in my daily life, gaining more self-knowledge, developing my strengths, and facing my challenges with wisdom. I say to myself and all present that I accept and integrate all that I am with honor and integrity as I strive to be the best I can be.*

Thank the beings you invoked for their assistance and close sacred space in your preferred manner.

This ritual is obviously written for the older child to perform alone. Younger children can be guided through it with a parent, but it is best if the child has some understanding of the energies associated with each direction before participating in such a ritual. Recording insights in a journal and celebrating with family and friends is the perfect end to this ritual.

As is true with any aspect of pagan spirituality, we can place the emphasis during home education on the academic, the magickal, or find a balance between both. However we choose to focus our studies, our children will gain a deeper understanding of themselves and the world through an exploration of the elements.

Resources

Books

Johnson, Cait and Maura D. Shaw (1995) *Celebrating the Great Mother.* Inner Traditions.

Madden, Kristin (2000) *Pagan Parenting.* Llewellyn

McArthur, Margie (1994) *Wiccacraft for Families.* Phoenix Publishing, Inc.

Starhawk, Diane Baker, Anne Hill (2000) *Circle Round.* Bantam

Web Sites

ExplorA-Pond
http://www.uen.org/utahlink/pond/

Give Water A Hand
http://www.uwex.edu/erc/gwah/
216 Agriculture Hall
1450 Linden Drive
Madison, WI 53706
800-928-3720
erc@uwex.edu

Japanese Kite Collection
Festivals, history and more
http://www.asahi-net.or.jp/~et3m-tkkw/

Sun
http://www.solarviews.com/eng/sun.htm

Sacred Grove and Tree Planting Programme
http://druidry.org/obod/intro/treeplanting.html

The Voice of the Woods
http://www.pixielations.com/ogham/index2.html

U.S. EPA Explorer's Club
http://www.epa.gov/kids/

U.S. EPA Curriculum Resources & Activities
http://www.epa.gov/teachers/curriculum_resources.htm

Weather Channel Education
http://www.weather.com/education/lounge/

Chapter Eight
Teaching through the Festivals

The eight holiday annual cycle is central to the Western neopagan tradition. Each year we follow the cycle of life and agriculture that coincides with the seasons, the cycles of day and night, and with our own life passages. Four of these ceremonies, often called the major sabbats by some Wiccan traditions, are based on the ancient Celtic festivals: Imbolc, Beltane, Lughnasadh, and Samhain. These are often referred to as the Fire festivals, but some scholars dispute this designation. The other four, known to modern druids as the Alban festivals and to many witches as lesser sabbats, are the equinoxes and solstices.

The Fire festivals were known to be agricultural and some say lunar-focused events. The solstices and equinoxes are obviously solar-based astronomical events. For ancient peoples, festivals were the high points of the year, full of markets, games, storytelling, and music. We can learn a great deal about the cultures and history of a people through an investigation of their holidays.

Each of these festivals takes place on or near similar festivals in various parts of the world. A unit study involving just one of the Celtic festivals can lead to an exploration of world-wide geography, history, and social studies through researching the other events taking place in a thirty-day period. You and your children will be amazed to see the similarities among festivals throughout the world.

With young children, this can be an introduction to changes that occur seasonally in the natural world in your area. Some changes will be obvious, but the cyclical nature of them will not be clear to very young children. Older children can dig more deeply into the scientific basis for these changes or the mythology of festivals.

Some families use these as opportunities to study different genres in literature and movies. I know a few families who incorporate a Health study into the festivals though learning about medicinal herbs that might be associated with each festival and preparing herbal medicines. Many families structure their Art, Music, and Home Economics (or Kitchen Witchery 101) around the seasonal festivals.

Through the observance of the festivals, we also bring to our lives a regularity of spiritual practice that continually reinforces our connection to the Gods and the world around us. We may not make every Moon phase or even every Full Moon, but in keeping to the eight annual holidays, we maintain an alignment to our spirituality and All That Is. This alone is a wonderful gift to give to a child.

Note on Location

It should be noted that the dates of these festivals are based on the northern hemisphere. Pagans in the southern hemisphere celebrate the festival opposite us on the Wheel of the Year. For example, when we celebrate Beltane, southern pagans are celebrating Samhain.

Note on Pronunciation

Rules of pronunciation vary with word origin, old or new variation, and local dialects. These words, heroes, and Deities are Welsh, Irish, Scottish, Gallic/Gaulish, or generally Celtic. However even within these areas, variations can alter pronunciation slightly to significantly. I offer an approximate phonetic spelling for any word that does not generally follow common American English phonetics.

Imbolc (*im-mulk*) -- February 2

The name of this festival literally means "in the belly." This is the time when seeds begin to stir in the belly of the Mother Earth and ewes give birth to lambs, leading to another name for this sabbat, Oimelc, meaning "milk of ewes." The former Scottish New Year, this is a time of new beginnings and the first visible signs of life after the winter.

As a festival of lights and Water, we often find floating candles on the altar for Imbolc. Our druid group used to surround a cauldron with white tapers. The cauldron held Water and floating candles. When toddlers were a part of the group they made it a point to go around and blow out all the tapers at least once during the ritual. It was great fun for everyone.

Many traditions associate the colors white and red with this festival. Snowdrops are common additions to Imbolc festivities. These white flowers have been called Candlemas Bells and the Purification Flower. Amethyst is the birthstone of February and many people use violets as the flower for this month.

An old rhyme, often attributed to the early Christians by way of the Romans, states that "If Candlemas Day be bright and clear, there'll be two winters in the year." On Groundhog Day, the story goes that if the groundhog comes out of his hole and sees its shadow, there will be another six weeks of winter. If it cannot see its shadow, which frightens it back underground, then spring is just around the corner. This season is an ideal time to investigate weather folklore and the origins of Groundhog Day.

Older children might be interested to find out that January and February were added to the Roman calendar several hundred years before the Common Era began. The name of February comes from a Latin word meaning "to purify." It is said that this word derives either from Februus, the ancient Roman God of purification and death or from the Goddess Februa, mother of Mars. Lupercalia was the Roman festival of purification in preparation for the coming spring festivals.

February is the shortest month with twenty-eight days and twenty-nine in leap years. This is a good time to learn the rhyme of the months that so many of us learned in compulsory school.

Thirty days hath September,
April, June, and November;
All the rest have thirty-one,
Excepting February alone
Which hath but twenty-eight, in fine,
Till leap year gives it twenty-nine.

Imbolc is the first of the three Spring festivals and is sacred to Brighid as Maiden Goddess. Brighid is the Goddess of poetry, smithcraft, Fire, and healing. She was associated with Minerva among the Romans and Athena among the Greeks. For the Christians, She became St. Brigid, Mary of the Gaels. This is an ideal time to start reading poetry or learning about healing.

This festival celebrates the first stirrings of seeds within the Earth. Starting seeds can provide you with an ideal lesson in plant biology and gardening science. Studies can carry over into energy experiments, nutrition or hydroponics experiments. You can incorporate history by researching the evolution of your plants and how they were used by people throughout time. Geography might be a nice addition if your plants are not native to your area or if they are widely exported, which also brings in a finance or economy aspect.

If your plants have medicinal properties or have been used for dyes or spells, you can incorporate additional biology and biochemistry, art and the science of dyes, and magick. Dorothy Morrison's *Bud, Blossom, and Leaf*[19] is a wonderful book that is equally applicable for a house plant "garden" as it is for those of us with outdoor gardens. I highly recommend it for any family who wants to incorporate some aspect of gardening or natural crafts into their home education.

If your children have begun to work with their own energy fields or energetic healing, a plant is an ideal subject for experimentation. This is also a good way to introduce the concept of biological energy that flows through the food web and its relationship to the energy we work with metaphysically. The idea is to approximate scientific method in your home by directly sending energy to one plant, talking to another without directing energy, and doing the basic care (Water and light) for a third. Any changes in the growth and development of the plant are recorded and compared to the others. The first thing to do is to start your seeds.

Sprouting Seeds

You will need:

- Something to sprout: seeds or dried beans[20] or lentils
- Wet paper towel
- Plastic bag
- Potting soil
- Pot with drainage holes at the bottom (peat pots can be transplanted directly into a garden)

To start your seeds sprouting, place them on the wet paper towel in the plastic bag. Keep in a warm, light place and do not completely close the plastic bag.

In a few days, you will see a sprout emerge from the seed. Allow it a few days to grow.

Then plant the seed in a pot about one-half inch below the surface of starter soil[21]. You can skip directly to this step without starting the seed in the bag, but that way you miss the fun of watching it begin to sprout.

When your plants grow to a few inches tall, you may want to transplant them into larger pots, depending on the type of plant. Keep in mind that fruits, such as strawberries, and vegetables, such as tomatoes, can be grown in containers for those without outdoor garden space.

Other February Events

In the U.S.A., this is Black History Month, celebrating and encouraging Americans to learn more about the accomplishments and contributions made by African Americans.

President's Day is celebrated in America on the third Monday in February, honoring the birthdays of George Washington and Abraham Lincoln

February 1: Candlemas. A Christian festival in the tradition of the light or Fire festivals. Churches bless candles and distribute them to the faithful.

February 2: St. Brigit's Day

February 2: Groundhog Day

February 3: Feast of the Purification of the Blessed Virgin Mary

February 2-5: Festival of the New Year in Tibet.

February 3: Setsubun, a Japanese festival marking the end of winter.

February 11: Thomas Edison's birthday

February 14: Valentines Day

February 15: Susan B. Anthony's birthday

Dates vary: Mardi Gras, Chinese New Year

Spring Equinox -- on or near March 21

For most people, this is the first day of spring. It is also called Vernal Equinox, Ostara, Eostre's Day, Alban Eiler (*Light of the Earth*), and the Festival of the Trees. Essential elements of this festival are the time of sowing and preparing to reap what has been sown. Alder trees are the harbingers of spring, blooming around the equinox. Other plants associated with this time of year are shamrocks and trefoil.

Children might enjoy a mythological survey of associated Deities and heroes of this holiday. The Saxon Eostre, Celtic Olwen and Niwalen, Greek Kore, Roman Persephone or Proserpina, and other Maiden Goddesses as well as the Green Man, Tammuz, and Osiris are all appropriate Deities to explore at this time. It is said that spring celebrations were also observed for Ishtar, Aphrodite, Hathor, and Kali. Historically, you might prefer to look into the lives of the Christian Saint Patrick or Alexander Graham Bell.

Legend tells us that this was the season of spring cleaning for the ancient Celts. Stories indicate that even the druids cleaned their temples at this time of year. Anyone with children knows that spring cleaning is an excellent idea. Children's rooms have a way of becoming black holes in which toys, books, shoes, and other things simply disappear. They tend to be found during a good cleaning and spring is as good a time as any for this.

The name of the Christian holiday Easter is derived from that of the Saxon fertility Goddess, Eostre. She was a Goddess of the Moon and Earth, whose symbols were the rabbit and the egg. It is largely thanks to her influence that we color eggs at this time of year. However, the tradition of egg-decoration is an intriguing unit study that can take you from North America through western and eastern Europe and beyond.

While you can purchase several commercial egg-coloring products, you might consider using natural dyes for your eggs. For each of the dyes below, boil Water (four quarts will color one dozen eggs) and add the "dye" until the color of the Water darkens. You may want to remove the plant material at this point. Add white vinegar (1/4 cup to 4 quarts Water) and your eggs. Refrigerate overnight and remove the eggs in the morning. This can be a fun project that may also lead into a study of the development of dyes around the world.

Natural Egg Dyes

- Orange: onion skins. Use more skins for a deeper color.
- Yellow: turmeric
- Red: peeled beets or beet juice
- Purple: sliced red cabbage: large quantity of inner leaves

- Light Blue: sliced red cabbage: small quantity of outer leaves
- Brown: use strong coffee in place of the Water

The spring equinox is an astronomical observance. Like the solstices and autumn equinox, this festival can provide an array of opportunities to study science and mythology. Equinox means "equal night." On the equinoxes, the northern and southern hemispheres of the Earth receive the same amount of sunlight. After the spring equinox, days will be longer than nights for people in the northern hemisphere until we reach the autumn equinox.

Many sacred sites around the world, including some early cathedrals, have been determined to be ancient astronomical observatories. Some measure what is known as the precession of equinoxes. This precession is a wobbling of the Earth's axis from the gravitational pull of the Sun and Moon. It causes the exact date of the festival to be altered. Myths, such as that of Mithra, have been said to contain information regarding the precession of equinoxes and the changing of our Pole Star.

This is also one of the two major migration seasons for birds, butterflies, and other creatures. Your children might be surprised to find out how many animals migrate, how far they go, and how they do this. Scientists don't know for sure how animals know just when to begin migration, but there are plenty of theories to investigate. General assumptions include seasonal changes in prey base and other food sources, along with changing light and temperatures. Studies have shown that birds use landmarks, Sun and star positions, and even the Earth's magnetic field for navigation as they migrate.

Some animals, like the Saw-whet Owl and some deer species, have a unique migration. They tend to migrate from higher to lower elevations, rather than between northern and southern sites. The Timber Rattlesnake will migrate between breeding and winter den sites. Some of winter dens may have been in use for hundreds, possibly thousands, of years.

Many migration dates and routes are incredibly regular. Swallows return to San Juan Capistrano each year on the equinox. Turkey Vultures head south on the autumnal equinox and return in the spring on the vernal equinox. They have frequently been documented returning to summer roosting sites on the exact day of the equinox. The regularity of migrations among reindeer, whales, and other large mammals has enabled native peoples to structure life around them. Sadly, this regularity has also enabled hunters to dramatically reduce some wild populations.

This can provide us with another mythology unit study, particularly regarding bird migration. The cyclic disappearance of birds was a mystery to our ancient ancestors. In some cultures, they were believed to travel to other worlds. Some people thought they hibernated in groups on the Moon or at the bottoms of lakes.

Other March Events

In the U.S.A., this is Women's History Month

March 3: Alexander Graham Bell's birthday

March 17: St. Patrick's Day

Dates vary: Purim, Easter day (after 1st Full Moon following spring equinox).

Beltane -- April 30- May 1

You may see the name of this festival spelled Beltain *(bell-tane)*, Bealteinne *(bee-ell-tin-ah)*, or other variations. However it is spelled, it means Bel's Fire. Bel or Belenos was a Fire God who has been associated with Apollo and Baal. It was customary in ancient Ireland for all Fires to be extinguished on Beltane Eve and relit from a Fire started at Tara by either the Druid or High King. Cattle were passed through two Fires (balefires) for protection and fertility. Young couples would also walk between Fires or jump the balefires for the same reasons.

Beltane is a time of love as many people begin to feel spring fever and the flowing of vital energy after a long winter. In Germany and Czechoslovakia, boys sometimes plant May trees or place maypoles in front of their sweethearts' windows at night. Italian men may serenade the women they love on this day. In Wales at this time, love spoons are carved from sycamore wood and given to the object of one's desire. Matches made at Beltane were often made official through handfasting at Lughnasadh.

Dancing around the Maypole and weaving together the brightly colored ribbons is a well-known custom on May Day. It reconnects communities and weaves us together as one people. This is often accompanied by Morris Dancers and the choosing of the May King and Queen. For some, the May Pole is a symbol of the joining of God and Goddess, as it is a phallic symbol planted in the Earth. For others, it is reminiscent of the World Tree that connects all worlds.

Balefires, or needfires, are a common tradition. Some people attempt to collect the nine sacred woods for their Fires. The list of nine woods varies with the source though, so many people prefer to use a variety of *ogham*[22] woods instead. This association with so many trees makes for a widely varied study plan. One can explore the myths of the trees, like the taboo on cutting a hawthorn tree except on May Day. You can also delve into the magickal aspects of woods, such as the use of rowan wood over the hearth or door to protect against enchantments. If you prefer a more traditional academic study, consider plant biology, logging methods and laws, or the Irish tree protection laws.

Making your own paper is not only a fun activity, but it also teaches children that they can take the Reuse-and-Recycle concept into their own hands by finding creative ways to do this. Homemade paper makes great gifts and you can use old office paper, worn out jeans, or even cardboard egg cartons for this project.

Home-made Paper

You will need:

- Bits of paper or cardboard torn into small pieces

- Screen with frame: window screening stapled to a picture frame will do
- Tub or bucket large enough to submerge the frame in
- Blender or food processor
- Sponge
- Stack of newspapers covered with a towel or other cloth
- Optional: iron for smoothing, liquid starch to prevent ink from soaking in too much when you write on it
- For color and texture: bleach, food coloring, pieces of leaves or flowers, etc.

Soak the bits of paper in hot Water for about thirty minutes.

Blend the soaked paper into a pulp until there are no pieces of paper left. Add optional bleach or coloring.

Fill the tub with Water and add the pulp in a ratio of four parts Water to one part pulp.

More pulp will make a thicker paper and you can experiment with this ratio. Mix this so the pulp is floating in the Water. If you want to use liquid starch, add one to two teaspoons now and mix well.

Submerge the screen in the tub. Slowly raise the screen to the top of the Water. Hold it just over the surface and allow most of the Water to drain. If you want a thicker or thinner paper, this is the time to add or remove pulp.

Carefully turn the screen over onto the stack of newspapers. Use the sponge to absorb as much Water as you can.

Gently lift the screen, removing the paper very carefully. If it sticks, it is either too wet or you pulled too quickly. Press out bubbles or tears.

Cover with another cloth and more newspaper for twenty-four hours. Remove new paper and allow it to dry for another twenty-four hours in a clean, dry place. Iron on low heat once it is fully dry.

An old rhyme tells us that April showers bring May flowers. Flowers are an integral part of any Beltane celebration, symbolizing the triumph of life over death and the returning spring to the world. In many parts of the world, this is an ideal time to take outdoor walks, looking for the first flowers and any other signs of life. This also promotes an awareness of the natural world in your local area.

Children who learn the native plants and the ways of wild creatures not only have a more intimate relationship with the Earth, but they gain confidence their survival abilities. These children know what plants to avoid and which ones provide medicine. They are truly aware and rarely get lost. However they know that if they need to, they can survive through wildcrafting.

Other May Events

May 1: Roodmas
May 5: Cinco de Mayo, Mexico
May 12: Florence Nightingale's birthday
Dates vary: Mother's Day, Memorial Day

Summer Solstice -- on or near June 21

Also known as Litha, Midsummer, Alban Heruin/ Hefin, this is the longest day and shortest night of the year. This is a time of rest following the spring planting and before the harvests to come. This solstice has historically been celebrated with a nightlong vigil and with hospitable feasts in many parts of the world.

The solstices have been marked by cultures around the world for thousands of years. In a time where electricity did not yet exist, the longest day could be expected to hold some importance. A study of ancient cultures, archeology, and archeoastronomy are quite appropriate for both solstices.

Many museum and educational stores sell kits that allow children to "dig" dinosaur bones in a mock archeological experiment. These are fun and usually come with informational materials, but they can be quite expensive. The cost may be enough to prevent families from doing this more than once or for those with several children from doing it at all. A mock dig is a fairly easy thing to set up at home. It can be done over and over and altered each time so it doesn't get redundant.

When choosing what to excavate, consider what you are studying, your children's interests, and their ages. Then see if you can come up with something appropriate. Families who cook full chickens or turkeys may have a clean skeleton to use. Museum supply and educational stores will also have plastic skeletons and other body parts.

Since bones are not the only things found in professional digs, you might consider burying a small cup or bowl. My son was so intrigued by the ancient South-western pottery when we visited Chaco Canyon that we decided to make our own pottery out of clay. We made a few extra pieces and buried these for our mock dig.

Kids' Dig

You will need:
- A sturdy box with a bottom, shoebox size or larger
- Something to excavate
- Sand or dirt: you might want to layer different types of dirt to simulate ground layers
- Excavation tools: shovels, brushes, plastic bags, labels, buckets, sieve or sifter, etc
- For older kids on a large dig: measuring tape, stakes, and string to divide up the area into equal squares for charting on graph paper

Make it a game by pretending that someone has just made an important discovery and your job is to excavate it for a museum. Explain how fragile these items may be and how careful you need to be on site. Show your children the tools they will be using and describe what each might be used for.

If you have older children working on a sand-box-sized or larger dig, help them to divide up the plot into squares of equal sizes, maybe a foot large. Use the string and stakes as dividers. Show them how to transfer their plots onto graph paper and record exactly where each item is found.

Let them dig and have as much fun with it as possible. Help them to label plastic bags and put the items in them for later examination. When you get back to the "lab," you can measure and weigh each piece and pretend to do carbon dating or an analysis of any plant material.

Make a model or draw a picture of the site you excavated, placing each item where it was found. Make hypotheses about the site, the people who used it, the time period, the climate, and anything else you can come up with.

**You might also consider creating fantasy digs simply to teach research, exploration, and hypothesizing skills. Pretending to be a space explorer, you might dig up pieces of spaceships or aliens. For a child with an interest in Pokemon or *Harry Potter*[23], you might dig up an ancient Dewgong from a desert that was once covered by ocean or a dragon's egg.

Midsummer's Eve is sacred to the Faerie folk. William Shakespeare illustrated this relationship in A Midsummer Night's Dream and this is a wonderful story for all ages. In the Aridian Tradition of Italian witchcraft, there is a festival, based on the feast of the Goddess Vesta from Roman times, honoring the fairies as Lare and Vesta as Queen of the Fairies.[24]

Most children love faery stories. Midsummer's Eve can be a fun time to have a bonfire and tell stories or sit outside and look for faeries. This is also a good time to study the plants associated with faery folk, such as rowan, rue, and fern, or to explore the faery stories from around the world. The similarities among cultural legends are impressive.

Other June Events

June 14: Flag Day, USA
Dates vary: Father's Day

Lughnasadh *(loo-nah-sah)* -- August 1

As the name implies, the Celtic God-hero Lugh is an important figure in the mythology of this first harvest festival, also known as Lammas or Loaf-Mass by the Christians. It is Lugh's feast day, yet it is equally a day honoring His foster mother Tailltiu *(tarl-too)*. She died clearing the forest of Brega to make fields for planting. To honor her, Lugh instructed the people of Ireland to gather for games and feasts on this day. Indeed, Olympic-style games were held at Tailltin, drawing people from all over Ireland.

Engaging in athletic contests and games, feasting, and all forms of merry-making are appropriate ways to celebrate this festival. This might be a good time to learn to juggle, ride a horse, or skate. You may prefer to practice crafting and sharing songs and stories. This was a time of great Fairs and if you have young entrepreneurs in your house, this would be an ideal time to launch a child's business. They can learn all about money, sales, banking, and more from a simple craft-selling business.

Young pagans can certainly enjoy running a summer lemonade stand, but you might also suggest that they make herb candles, paper, incense, or other items that might be of interest to local metaphysical shops. Many shops will take things like this on consignment and the fact that it is a child's project may be just the right selling point.

In ancient times, this was the time for handfastings. Romantic matches begun at Beltane or other times of the year were frequently made official on Lughnasadh. The handfasting traditionally lasted for one year and one day, allowing the couple to make an informed decision about making this a permanent pairing. Unlike the more conservative mainstream religions, pagan traditions have no taboos on living together before marriage. In fact, many pagans agree that it is a good idea before becoming legally obligated to someone. Lughnasadh may be an ideal opportunity to discuss these matters with your older children.

Lughnasadh is also the first of the grain harvests and the time for making breads. This is also where the name of Lammas or Loaf-Mass comes from. Bread making does take patience, but it is a wonderful thing to teach your children. There is nothing quite like eating a bread made by your own hands and blessed with pure ingredients and loving energy.

I prefer mixed-grain bread and tend to add whole grains whenever our son Karl isn't looking. Karl always wants to add something more fun, like raisins, blueberries, or even molasses to make it a little bit more like his favorite pumpernickel. This recipe is an excellent basic one that does not require waiting for it to rise and punching it down. It is also perfect for experimentation and addition of fun ingredients.

Harvest Bread

You will need:
- 1 cup whole oats
- 1 cup whole wheat flour
- 1 cup oat bran
- 1/2 tsp salt
- 1 tsp cinnamon
- 1/4 tsp nutmeg
- 1 cup milk
- 1 tsp baking soda
- 1/2 cup honey
- optional herbs such as rosemary, basil
- optional additions such as raisins, cheese, cranberries, etc

Preheat oven to 350 degrees Fahrenheit. Grease a bread loaf pan with olive oil or butter.

Mix in one bowl: oats, flour, oat bran, salt, cinnamon, and nutmeg. If you are adding herbs, cheese, or fruit, add to this bowl.

Mix in another bowl: milk, baking soda, and honey

Combine both bowls, mixing until dry ingredients are moist.

Pour into pan and bake for approximately one hour, until a toothpick inserted into the center comes out clean.

Cool for ten minutes. Remove from pan and allow to cool for another ten minutes before serving.

In honor of the grain harvest, mythology studies might focus on Goddesses like Demeter, Ceres, and the

Native American Corn Mother or on John Barleycorn in addition to Lugh and other Gods of light. Odin (*Oh-thin*) is also appropriate for this season, since it is said that He hung himself on the Yggdrasil, the ash tree, to obtain rune knowledge in mid-August. Artio the Celtic Bear Goddess was honored at this time, as were the dry-ads in Macedonia.

Other August Events

August 6: first atomic bomb: dropped by USA on Hiroshima, Japan
August 19: Orville Wright's birthday
August 21: Hawaii becomes 50th US state

Autumn Equinox -- on or near September 21

Another astronomical observance, the autumn equinox, has been marked since ancient times. This date is known to neopagans as Mabon and Alban Elfed/Elued. As an equinox, we focus on balance as night and day are equal. From this date forward, darkness is on the increase as nights grow longer.

For many, this is a time of thanksgiving and our modern Thanksgiving celebrations arose from the harvest feasts of the early Europeans. We give thanks for the harvests and all our blessings as we prepare for the coming winter.

With winter approaching, this was often a time of weather forecasting and a great many folklore traditions arose from the need to find some way to determine how long and hard the winter would be. Many of these customs seem like mere superstition, yet they are frequently based in sound observation and applied science. This is a fun and intriguing study for many of us, young and old alike.

Weather Folklore[25]

- A long, hot summer indicates a windy autumn
- A windy autumn precedes a mild winter
- The first frost in autumn will be exactly six months after the first thunderstorm of the spring.
- It will be a long and hard winter if:
  - wooly bear caterpillars are more black than brown.
  - squirrels gather and bury their nuts early
  - trees produce an abundance of nuts.
  - the leaves fall late
  - apple skins are tough
  - cornhusks are thick
  - onion skins are thick
  - birds migrate early
  - fruit trees bloom in the fall
  - the breastbone of a fresh-cooked turkey is dark purple

One of the most amazing aspects of autumn is the changing of leaves. Leaf watching is so popular that newscasts and web sites publish peak viewing times and families travel far and wide to see the glorious colors. While younger children can understand the changing colors on a very basic level, the science of this season is best left to older kids.

The energies of the harvest and the end of the food-producing season are not only manifested on the land and in the skies, but on much smaller levels as well. During the spring and summer, the leaves of plants and stalks of grasses function to produce food for the rest of the plant. This food production occurs in the cells that contain chlorophyll, the pigment that gives these types of plants their green color.[26]

Other pigments, not visible in spring and summer because of the abundance of chlorophyll, are responsible for the beautiful colors. As temperatures drop and daylight shortens, chlorophyll breaks down. This allows the other pigments to emerge and chemical changes to occur, bringing forth the yellows, oranges, reds, and even deep purples of the season.

An exploration of the effects of Water and temperature on leaf colors will often lead into a study of the various trees and their colors. This is another excellent time to work with Tree energy and investigate plant biology as well as the traditional uses for trees, like syrup from maples and drums from cottonwoods. Irish law protects certain species of trees and categorizes them. It is interesting to note that even in American history, special trees hold important stories for us, like Boston's Liberty Elm.

This equinox is another ideal time to look into archeoastronomy. From ancient observatories found throughout the world, we learn that our ancestors had complex astronomical and mathematical knowledge. We also gain a recognition of the importance these solar events held for ancient peoples.

While many of these sites were created to mark a variety of astronomical events, some focused on eclipses, other stars, solstices, or equinoxes. In Mexico at the Mayan pyramid in Chichen Itza, equinox sunrise and sunset lights up the northern stairway, making it appear to be a snake, sliding up and down the pyramid. Ancient structures at Macchu Pichu in Peru are designed to measure the precession of the equinoxes.

In the United States, Chaco Canyon holds some of the most amazing ruins in the country. The Anasazi people built the Sun Dagger there. On the equinox at local noon, sunlight makes a dagger shape on a spiral on the far wall. In this same huge complex is Casa Rinconada. This includes one of the largest kivas, usually subterranean ceremonial structures in the country. It is precisely aligned to the solstices and equinoxes. Scholars believe that the entire Chacoan complex was built in alignment with astronomical events.

Similar sites are found through the British Isles, into Israel, and as far away as New Zealand. This gives us clues as to the importance of these events among ancient peoples. It also informs us about the complex knowledge possessed by our species so long ago. These places have equally rich mythology and a study of these cultures and their beliefs should prove to be a fascinating one.

Other September Events

In the U.S.A., this is Native American Month and Hispanic Heritage Month

September 15: Michaelmas

September 26: John Chapman's (Johny Appleseed) birthday

September 28: Harriet Tubman took her parents to safety

Dates vary: Labor Day, Grandparent's Day, Rosh Hashanah, Yom Kippur

Samhain (*sah'wen or sow-een*) -- around October 31

Everyone knows this festival best as Halloween. It is All Hallow's Day, All Saint's Eve, and has been called the Celtic New Year. Traditional Celtic celebrations took place for three days in late October and early November. Our modern Halloween traditions of dressing up in costume probably derive from the old Celtic view of this time of "no-time" when the Veil between worlds was thin involving planned craziness and dressing up. People would wear clothes backward and men would dress as women in some areas.

For several cultures, including many neopagan traditions, this is the Festival of the Dead: the time to honor our ancestors and departed loved ones. As such, this is a wonderful time to talk to your children about their families. Older children might like to start delving into genealogy and researching their family tree. Even young children enjoy seeing the names of parents, grandparents, siblings, and cousins on a simple family tree that they can help write or decorate.

If your children are still very young, you might want to use this time of year to start recording information about your family. Help older children learn to scrapbook or even videotape the stories of family members. If your family elders are still alive, ask them to tell you and your children stories of the family and how life was when they were younger. Encourage them to give as many names, places, and dates as possible as they share colorful stories, feelings, and dreams. This bonding with elders is a beautiful experience for children and adults alike. Because this is sadly lacking in many modern cultures, it is an equally powerful gift of honor for your elders.

Find out where your family is from, if possible. Use this personal interest to motivate an exploration of the history, geography, culture, and languages of the areas your ancestors were from. Even if you have adopted children and do not know their biological heritage, or just don't know where your family is from, you can begin to record your family's information now. You are the ancestors for future generations. Taking the time to label photographs and keep family journals could prove invaluable to your descendants.

Of course, we all connect Samhain or Halloween and pumpkins. Pumpkin carving and cooking all sorts of pumpkin foods are part of the joy of this season. Growing your own pumpkins is a great project, but you will need to plant in the summer for a fall harvest. For children who don't like to eat vegetables, this is the ideal growing project if you have the time. This is a plant that they can actually use after the harvest and it is much more fun than just eating it.

As the pumpkin grows, children learn about gardening science and possibly a little magick as well. They can see the life stages of the plant and how the fruit develops. They can investigate the squash family and the history of pumpkin use. Then when it comes time to carve out the jack-o-lantern, they can a first-hand look at the inside of the fruit. Children can find the meat, the seed, and see how the skin protects all that. The meat may be used in foods depending on the type of pumpkin and the seeds can always be roasted or dried to eat later.

Halloween is also associated with things like bats, spiders, ghosts, and skeletons, among other things. Although everyone likes to tell scary stories sometimes, we can diminish the fear of these things by learning and talking about them. In addition to scientific or cultural studies of bats and spiders, we can discuss them as power animals and spirit guides. Ghosts can be distinguished from true spirits and ancestors by making it clear that they are created for scary stories.

Skeletons can provide a wide array of study subjects. This can begin with young children by singing the skeleton song about the arm bone connected to the shoulder bone, and so on. This is a good teaching song for helping very young children learn body parts. Older children can expand on the skeleton study by learning the function and form of the skeleton; how it connects to muscles and how one's diet affects bones. A study like this can lead an interested child into an investigation of osteoporosis or a comparative study of the anatomy and physiology of vertebrates and invertebrates.

Make A Skeleton

You will need:

- Diagram or model of the skeleton for the species you want to recreate
- Bones: cotton swabs, small sticks, or white strips of paper
- Glue or transparent tape
- Piece of cardboard or dark construction paper for background
- Optional: clear plastic sheets, colored markers, and a diagram of muscle systems, organs, or the chakra system.

Begin with the backbone of the skeleton you are creating and glue or tape the necessary pieces to the background.

Follow the diagram or model and build your skeleton onto the backbone. Label or record the name and function of as many bones as you can.

Optional: create a model of the muscles or organs of the body on the clear plastic paper by drawing it on the plastic sheets. This may be overlaid on the skeleton for a more complete view of the physical body.

Optional: create a model of chakras and aura on the clear plastic paper by drawing it with markers on the plastic sheets. This may be overlaid on the physical body for a more complete view of the total being.

Other October Events

October 24: United Nations Day
October 28: Statue of Liberty dedicated
Dates vary: Sukkot

Winter Solstice -- around 21 December

A great old holiday carol calls this the most wonderful time of the year. For many people, it is just that. There is so much to do between holiday shopping, decorating, watching holiday shows on television, and in many areas, all manner of snow play. This time of year brings with it an excitement that is rarely surpassed by another holiday season.

Much of this excitement is spurred by the common perception of this as a big gift-giving season. Many children in pagan families, like some Jewish families I know, celebrate their own religious festivals as well as Christmas. For many people, Christmas has become so secular and commercial, plus the fact that it is obviously based in pagan celebrations, it is not seen as a religious conflict to celebrate it.

Even those who object to the celebration of Christmas unless you are Christian, this season is still full of fun. Between Solstice and New Year's Eve, there are parties and rituals and shopping to fill your schedule. For the crafty home educator, there are innumerable activities to do, many of which can produce wonderful gifts for loved ones.

Evergreens are a common decoration at this time

of year. This tradition dates back at least five hundred years, possibly several thousand. The evergreen is a tree that retains its "leaves" and stays green all year round.

Also known as Yule and Alban Arthuan, this is the season of the child of light. This is when the Great Mother gives birth to Jesus, Mithras, Horus, and others as the Sun symbolically dies and is reborn. After this longest night, the light increases in our world as days grow longer. Because of this association with returning light, this is a Fire festival and people around the world often celebrate it with candles and Fires.

The Yule Log is a favorite tradition in many homes. In some traditions this should be of oak while in others it is of birch. It is decorated with other woods, such as holly and ivy, along with ribbons or symbols of the season. It is customary for a small portion of the Yule log to be kept unburned. It provides protection for the home throughout the year and brings a sense of continuity through the Wheel as it is added to the next year's Fire and burned with the new Yule Log.

There is another type of Yule Log that can be used year after year. This is a small log with two or three candle-sized holes drilled in it. It is decorated with fresh greens each year and bayberry candles are burned in it for prosperity and abundance in the new year. Other candles can be substituted for bayberry if you prefer.

Yule Log

You will need:

- A branch approximately twelve inches long and thick enough to hold the candles you will use
- Sharp, strong knife or wide drill bit and drill
- Fresh evergreens
- Optional: glue
- Other decorations, such as red or gold ribbons, holly berries, mistletoe with berries, foil suns
- Candles

Carve or drill holes to hold your candles. Measure the candles you intend to use on the branch so they fit properly.

Tie with ribbon or glue the greens and other decorations to the branch, leaving space for the candles.

Add the candles.

Thank the trees that gave the branch and greens and bless your Log in sacred space.

Lighting the candles, chant something like this:

Branch of green, branch of light,
Bless us now and burn so bright.
Yule Log from the sacred tree,
Bring us health and prosperity.

Other December Events

December 12: Feast of Our Lady of Guadelupe
December 13: St. Lucia's Day
December 16: Las Posadas
December 25: Christmas
December 26: Kwanzaa
December 31: secular Western New Year
Dates vary: Hanukkah, Ramadan

This is but a small overview of the possibilities inherent in using the neopagan festivals as teaching opportunities. Each family will find their own lessons as individual interests and family traditions lead them. You can use this chapter to guide an exploration of the Norse festivals or holidays in other countries and religions.

Not only do the festivals offer us an opportunity to renew connections to community and the cycles of the natural world, they also provide us with a chance to learn and have fun with family. As home educators, this translates into a continual supply of new or expanded unit studies every few months. It can make it very easy on those of us that plan curricula for the year. Thanks to the Wheel of the Year, we have a specific variety of themes to choose from at certain times. This only deepens our children's understanding of the seasons and their connection to the Gods. In truth, taking part in this type of exploration can also deepen a parent's understanding and connection as well.

Recommended Reading

Amber K and Azrael Arynn K (2001) *Candlemas.* Llewellyn

Campanelli, Pauline and Dan (1989) *Wheel of the Year.* Llewellyn.

Carr-Gomm, Philip, ed. (1996) *The Druid Renaissance* Thorsons, HarperCollins

Carr-Gomm, Philip (1997) *The Elements of the Druid Tradition.* Element Books.

Franklin, Anna (2002) *Midsummer.* Llewellyn

Franklin, Anna and Paul Mason. (2001) *Lammas.* Llewellyn

Grimassi, Raven (2001) *Beltane.* Llewellyn

Hutton, Ronald, (1993) *The Pagan Religions of the Ancient British Isles, their Nature and Legacy.* Blackwell Publishers

Johnson, Cait and Maura D. Shaw (1995) *Celebrating the Great Mother.* Inner Traditions.

Madden, Kristin (2002) *Mabon.* Llewellyn

McCoy, Edain (2002) *Ostara.* Llewellyn

Morrison, Dorothy (2000) *Yule*. Llewellyn

Ravenwolf, Silver (1999) *Halloween*. Llewellyn

Starhawk, Diane Baker, Anne Hill (2000) *Circle Round*. Bantam

Online Resources

Mything Links
http://www.mythinglinks.org

Ord Brighideach
http://www.ordbrighideach.org

Thursdays Classroom: lesson plans and educational activities from NASA
http://www.thursdaysclassroom.com/index_23sep99.html

Skulls Unlimited: ethical supplier of museum-quality fakes and some real-bone animal parts
http://www.skullsunlimited.com
or call 1-800-659-SKULL for a print catalog

Chapter Nine
Magick and Ritual

Unless you are actively training a young priest or priestess, you may question what role magick and ritual could play in home education. The truth is that these are integral parts of the lives of most people, spiritual and religious people in particular. Graduation ceremonies are a ritual. Prayer is a form of magick. Anything that we do to effect change in our lives can be considered a form of magick, especially when it involves energy or beings outside the normal range of experience.

As neopagans, we use ritual, divination, and spellwork to gain insight and to effect change in our lives. As home educators, we provide our children with more tools for success and self-knowledge when we teach them about magick and ritual. Not only that, but we pave the way for deeper bonding as a family when we work together in sacred space.

Divination

The use of divination methods can play a surprisingly important role in the life of a child, even one as young as three. Consider how you use the tools that are familiar to you. Ask your favorite tarot reader, astrologer, or palmist what types of things they focus on when reading for themselves or their loved ones. Chances are good that simple "fortune" telling is not the major focus of divination.

For children, divination can serve as many purposes as it does for adults. Through divination, children can gain self-knowledge at an early age. As I wrote earlier, with an ability to really know their own motivations, fears, strengths, and weaknesses, children develop a control over their own life experience that most of adults still strive toward. When a child is experiencing resistance or having difficulty in a certain subject area, families can use divinatory tools to uncover the reasons behind the issues and find a way through them.

When children are uncomfortable or have a fight with someone, they have the tools available to uncover the reasons for their feelings and actions. They are also able to gain some insight into the reasons behind the conflict. Armed with knowledge, they can begin to work through their shadows and create life from a clearer state of being.

With so many societal blocks to trusting intuition and maintaining one's faith in spirit guides, the use of divinatory tools can boost a child's self-confidence and faith in the flow of energy through our world and others. With each success, their trust in their own intuition and abilities to find their own answers is supported. While having fun, they are encouraged to develop, rather than give up or block, their innate magickal abilities.

The following are some of the easiest yet most powerful methods that can be taught to any child old enough to understand verbal direction and formulate a question. Teens can obtain particular benefit from the use of these methods because of their distinctive state of energetic, emotional, and hormonal flux.

Pendulums

I learned to use the pendulum when I was nine. My son learned just after his fifth birthday. It is so simple that children as young as three have learned to use it with success. It is also ideal for the young child because it is simple and does not require any breakable tools. Anything strung on a rope or chain will suffice. We have used rings, crystals, and necklaces, as well as formal, weighted pendulums.

Since a pendulum can only make so many unique movements, it is best to use questions requiring only "yes" or "no" responses, at least in the beginning. As your children grow older and get more experienced with this method, their questions and the expected responses can become fairly complex.

Hold the chain a few inches above the pendulum, allowing it to hang freely. You may rest your arm on your other arm or on a few books if necessary. Take a deep breath and relax your body and mind. Visualize all tensions and attachments to the answer flowing out of you into the Earth. If your children feel a connection to spirit guides or Deities, it may help to ask for the assistance of these beings in this work.

Ask the pendulum to show you the "yes" and "no"

responses. These will usually be either a circular motion in one specific direction or a side-to-side motion. Each should be distinctive enough to prevent misunderstandings. Allow enough time for your body and mind to relax so the answers can flow through you and the pendulum.

Once you have determined these responses, you may ask your questions. If the answers are unclear, try rephrasing the question to be clearer. As your children gain experience with this tool, they may ask for more complicated responses, even using charts to gain specific answers. These can be created in either circles or half-circles, divided into spaces. Each space represents an answer and direction for the pendulum to move into, giving a definite response according to the chart.

Kinesiology

My mother first introduced my son to this technique when he was five. She and I were using it to find an owl that had decided to hide in my office. Karl watched us for a while then asked if our arms had special magick. The technique made great sense to him and he has used it successfully ever since, even insisting that we hold out an arm when he wants answers.

The basic idea is that the body-mind knows what the analytical mind may not be ready to acknowledge. This is also known as muscle testing because it is based on the immediate strength or weakness of the arm muscles. To use this, all you need is a friend's arm and a question. You may need to play with the question a bit to make it clearer if the answer is vague, so this may require adult assistance at the younger ages.

Have your assistant hold out an arm. They may hold it out to the side or out in front, depending on what feels right for you. The assistant is to hold the arm strongly up against any resistance from you. Before asking your question, ask what the "yes" and "no" responses are, pushing down on the arm with each question. You will most likely get a strong arm for a "yes" and at least an initial lowering of the arm for a "no." It is the initial, immediate response that indicates the answer.

Once you have established the responses, repeat the same process with your specific question. When the question is emotionally charged, many people like to ask if it is ok to even ask the question or if an accurate response can be determined with the assistant at hand. The value in kinesiology is that it bypasses the rational mind so thoroughly that emotion-driven responses are rarely a factor.

Tarot

Tarot can be an involved discipline requiring years of practice and study to fully understand. Even adults need to refer back to the deck booklet for meanings and spreads. Yet children seem to intuitively reach into the images on the cards and bring forth an astounding depth of understanding.

This works best with a deck that attracts the individual child. When my son was very young, he wanted to "play" with cards like I did so I gave him my old *Herbal Tarot Deck* (U.S. Games, 1988). He liked it and learned a bit from it, but it wasn't until *The Celtic Dragon Tarot* (Llewellyn, 1999) came out that Karl really connected with this system.

These images were very real to my then three-year-old son. In them, he saw not only the descriptions and many of the meanings offered in the book but applications that completely surprised me. He was able to pick a card for all the people in his life and they were truly accurate, almost embarrassingly so sometimes. Furthermore, he learned that if he asked his deck a question and sent that question into the cards, he could get his answer with a very simple spread we created together.

When teaching people to use a new deck, I always begin by guiding them to get to know the deck before actually reading the intended meanings. This is the same technique that I have found works well with children from age two to teens. We go through the cards one by one. If the child is unable to write, a parent writes down the images and feelings the child immediately associates with each card. This becomes a supplement to the book that accompanies a deck. As the child gets older, these meanings are deepened or expanded upon.

With practice, a relationship develops that is highly personal. The cards become almost like an extension of the child. There is no thought or analysis necessary in readings since the child innately knows what the deck is saying. Several of the children I have worked with keep the same deck into the teenage years. Even though they may add decks to their working collection, many of these young people will go to that first deck that they know so well for confirmation or really important readings.

Tarot also provides home educators with a tool similar to flashcards from which games and learning examples can be derived. We have played addition games with the minor arcana and used all the cards to practice reading. Both my son and I have learned something about herbs from one deck and about animals and their legends from another deck. Each of these decks served as the base for a full unit study on certain herbs or animals that caught his attention.

School Magick

Magick for school can take a variety of forms. It may manifest through spells and rituals, but it can also be seen in meditations and other methods of trance work. In school, we use magick to facilitate the learning process, help us access memory and retrieve facts, and assist in clearing the mind to more easily work through problems.

When I was young, I remember asking my mother if this was cheating. I wanted to know if it was fair for me to get the answers from the teacher's energy field or with the assistance of spirit guides. She answered me by asking if I planned to go through life sealing off that aspect of myself.

She said that if reading body language and tone of voice was not cheating then using other natural senses and reading energy fields was not cheating. She pointed out that, whether we are aware of it or not, much of what we do comes from intuition and spirit guidance. We are not isolated beings, relying on our own personal power, unless we choose to be. The only difference with magick is that we maintain a conscious knowledge of that connection to All of Life.

When it comes to home education, magick is simply the development of yet another ability for success, like networking. Most of us do not cast spells to get us great SAT scores in spite of the fact that we haven't bothered to learn the material. We work toward developing personal strengths and clearing the way for our natural abilities to shine through.

One note about all the exercises and spells in this chapter: these should be done within sacred space. Parents should hold the energy and create a ritual atmosphere for any child who is not able to create sacred space on their own.

Magick Mirror

This is designed to assist you in purifying unwanted aspects of self and manifesting your goals.

You will need:

- An unused mirror that can be devoted solely to magick
- Rubbing alcohol and a clean cloth
- Oil of sandalwood or jasmine
- One red cloth and one black cloth, large enough to completely cover the mirror

Thoroughly clean the mirror and frame with rubbing alcohol and allow it to dry in the Sun if possible.

Allow yourself at least twenty minutes when you can be alone and undisturbed.

Sit and gaze into the mirror. See yourself for all that you are. Holding the black cloth, allow those aspects of yourself that you want to eliminate to come up. These may be physical, emotional, spiritual, or mental. See these things very clearly in the mirror. Exaggerate them if you need assistance making them the main focus of your reflection.

Clean the surface once more with rubbing alcohol. Then, anointing the frame with essential oil, say out loud, "I lovingly release these things. They no longer serve me and do not benefit my chosen goals. Be Gone!"

Quickly cover the mirror with the black cloth.

Call upon your spirit guides and any Deities you believe will assist you in manifesting what you desire. Holding the red cloth, ask for their blessings as you imagine yourself already embodying these things. Pretend or visualize yourself in the way you want to be. When you can really see and feel this, uncover the mirror and place the black cloth a few feet away from you.

Still holding the red cloth, maintain those feelings as you look into the mirror. See yourself renewed and changed. Close your eyes if you need to in order to hold onto that new image of yourself. Cover the mirror with the red cloth.

Bury or burn the black cloth to release the old image and feelings about yourself.

For three days, sit with the mirror for seven minutes and hold only the new image of yourself, sending that energy into the mirror.

Knowledge Anchor[27]

This is a physical spell we cast on our own bodies. It instills an anchor in the form of a *mudra*, or sacred hand position, that creates an immediate access to memory or intuition.

Before beginning the exercise, decide on a hand position that is easily attainable but not something you will do on a regular basis without thinking about it. You might touch the ring finger and pinkie to your palm or bring your thumb and middle finger together.

Drum yourself into a light trance. If you do not use the drum, count yourself down from ten to one, twice. It may help for you to visualize yourself descending one step with each number.

Become aware of your breathing. Observe it for a few moments. If you still feel any areas of tension, direct the breath to these areas until they relax.

Now, begin to increase the duration of your exhalation until you have attained a 1:2 ratio between inhalation and exhalation. If you find you are gasping for breath on the inhalation, reduce the length of the exhalation. This should flow naturally without creating stress. Stay with the breath until you feel your trance deepen.

Place your hands in the position you have decided will be your physical anchor. Take a deep breath and focus completely on this anchor. Feel the physical sensation, the skin against skin, the pressure, whatever it is that this posture feels like.

Allow your focus to expand to include your trance and the energy of the room. Feel this energy create the anchor and feel the anchor create this energy. They are bound; integrated parts of one complete experience. Breathe into this feeling.

If you want to create more specific associations with this anchor, such as the experience of succeeding at a task or the feeling of opening to spirit guides, bring those elements into your ritual now, while holding the anchor position. Call up the memory of success or call in the Deity to evoke the experience of whatever it is that you want to occur automatically when this anchor is activated.

Once again, allow your focus to expand to include your trance and the energy of the room as you felt it during this last step. Feel this energy create the anchor and feel the anchor create this energy. They are bound; integrated parts of one complete experience. Breathe deeply into this feeling.

Tensing the anchor position, say to yourself and to those you have invoked, that this position will automatically create these conditions in your energy field whenever you take this position. State with intent that you will automatically assume this position without conscious thought whenever you have need of these conditions. State that this physical posture anchors these conditions in your physical body. Repeat this twice.

Ask the assistance and guidance of those you have invoked in deepening this anchor. Thank them for their presence and blessings and release the sacred space in your preferred manner.

*Make it a point to use this anchor each time you create similar conditions, perform your chosen meditation, or invoke your spirit guides. Continue to do this until you feel it becoming automatic.

Working with the Moon

Even young children can be guided to work with the phases of the Moon, providing for a monthly cycle of beneficial magick. Aligning with the energy of each phase helps energies to flow smoothly. As discussed in chapter six, families can use this to spur discussions about working with natural energies rather than trying to work against them or pretending they do not exist.

The New Moon is the time to work for new beginnings, focusing on personal growth and healing. This is a good time to begin new projects, start new studies, or make the jump into a new grade level. If there are specific strengths children want to develop or energies you would like to bring into your home education experience, the New Moon is the time to sow those seeds.

While the Moon is waxing, it appears to grow in the sky and people work growing, constructive magick. This is the time for growing things and developing strengths. The waxing is a good period to develop creativity and bring the knowledge obtained during any Dark Moon meditations into everyday life.

The Full Moon can be a difficult time to for some people as everything seems to come to a head. This is an intense period of time when the energies around you and anything you have sown in earlier phases comes to fruition. It is a good time to work for protection.

Many people will build a cone of power in circle and release it by yelling and sending it out. This is a Full Moon type of activity. All the energy from the New Moon builds until the Full. If you are sowing seeds of balance or grounding, the Full Moon will be a productive period. But if you are unbalanced or scattered, the Full Moon can bring with it excessive emotions, mood swings, and a general unpleasant feeling.

The Full Moon is a good time to focus on those things that make you uncomfortable or present blocks to the attainment of your goals. This is a good time to reevaluate curriculum goals and clarify feelings regarding certain subjects or methods. For some people, this is a time of heightened psychic abilities. For others, it is an external time of outward contact and often higher sexuality.

During the Moon's waning phase, She seems to shrink in the sky, and this reflects the type of magick associated with this time. This is period of release and banishing. It is a time to let go of what no longer serves you and prepare to complete the cycle begun at the New Moon. If there are blocks to success or energies you feel do not work for your homeschooling, this is the time to get rid of them.

At the Dark Moon, She is hidden from us for three days prior to the New Moon. This is often a time of going within, working with intuition, and calling for vision. Now is a good period to work on developing greater self-knowledge and getting to the core of anything that is causing concern or making you uncomfortable. This is another good time to work to eliminate bad habits or unwanted energies. For many people, this is the time of highest psychic influence and divination is particularly productive at this time.

These general energies of the Moon phases are also influenced by the sign the Moon is in during the phase. Moon magick can be made even more powerful if you consider the element of the current zodiac sign. If the Moon is in an Air sign when She is New, you might consider focusing your energy on inspiration or intellectual pursuits. If She is in a Water sign at the Dark, work on emotional insight or healing.

New Moon Magickal Bread

to increase memory and mental powers

You will need:

- 1 cup local honey
- 1/3 cup butter
- 2 eggs
- 1 1/2 cup applesauce
- 1/4 cup Water
- 1 2/3 cups flour
- 1 tsp baking soda
- 1/2 tsp salt
- 1 tsp baking powder
- 1 tablespoon rosemary
- 1/4 cup walnuts, chopped

Preheat the oven to 350 degrees Fahrenheit and grease a round baking pan with a small amount of butter.

Mix the butter, honey, eggs, and applesauce until well blended.

Stir in all other ingredients and pour into the pan.

Have everyone place their hands on the bowl and visualize themselves with improved memory and increased mental abilities as you all chant:

> *Walnut, apple, and rosemary,*
> *Grant our wish for better memory*

Bake approximately one hour, until a toothpick or sharp knife inserted into the center comes out clean.

Cool for ten minutes and remove from pan.

Gather everyone together before cutting the bread. Have them hold hands in a circle. Those on either side of you will place their hands on your shoulders. If there are only two of you, have the child hold out hands with palms open over the bread with you.

Holding your hands, palms open, over the bread, bless it with increased memory and mental abilities, as well as any specific energies you desire. Give thanks to the Gods as you cut the bread for their continued blessings in your life.

Full Moon Fire Magick

to release blocks to success

You will need:

- A cauldron or fire-proof container and matches or a lighter
- White paper and a pencil
- Cinnamon and ginger
- Optional: sagebrush and sweetgrass

Draw a picture or write down on the paper what

you want to clear and release.

Placing the cinnamon and ginger in the center, fold the paper three times.

Hold the paper in your hands and picture the feelings or situations you want to release this. Encourage children to really get into this by bringing up pictures, feelings, memories, and more. Send all that energy into the paper.

Ask the Goddess of the Moon and the sacred herbs in your paper packet to help clear you of these energies. Ask Their blessings as you work to eliminate this from your life.

You may want to light some sagebrush and sweetgrass in the cauldron now and place the paper on top of this Fire for additional assistance in purification and bringing in preferred energies. Otherwise, simply light the paper on Fire.

Visualize the energies being released by the Fire and passed on to the Gods in the smoke.

Rites of Passage

We are all familiar with rites of passage for birth and death. Many pagans also perform Namings or adulthood rites, particularly for girls who have begun to menstruate. Graduation can be seen as a rite of passage but unless a homeschooling family designs a graduation ceremony for family and friends, homeschoolers rarely experience that rite.

In this chapter, I detail a graduation rite along with both male and female adulthood rituals. The graduation rite can altered to fit any form of "graduation." It has been the basic outline for the graduation from diapers to underwear and for major milestones in a home educated child's life. It can also serve as the base outline for a Leaving the Nest ritual, before a child moves out of the family home or goes away to college.

Graduation

This ritual is written for a family celebrating a "middle" or "high" school graduation. However, it can be altered or simplified to suit a graduation from any "grade" or apprenticeship.

The ritual leader will need to create some form of quest for the graduating child before the ritual takes place. A series of appropriate clues should be developed for the child to follow during the ritual. This need not be a difficult or extensive quest. Its purpose is a ritual enactment of the quest for learning and the attainment of the goal.

Set up altar:

- Altar cloth: white, yellow, deep blue, or violet
- White and yellow or purple candles
- Clear quartz and amethyst
- Salt and warm Water
- Symbols of the student's helping spirits or Deities
- Symbols of the course of study
- Quest clues
- Certificate of graduation

Smudge each other before entering the circle.

Cast the circle and consecrate it with smudge and Water.

Ritual Leader invokes the directions:

I give thanks for the blessings of
Earth, Air, Fire, and Water.
Guide us and guard us in this ritual.
Lend us Your energies, now and forever,
That our every action may honor You.

Ritual Leader invokes the God and Goddess and any spirit guides who should be present:

Dear Ones,
We honor Your presence in our lives.
We are grateful for Your guidance
and assistance in this journey.
As this child graduates
and enters a new chapter of life,
We ask Your blessings and protection for her/him.
Guard us all and guide our steps
That we may all live a full and honorable life
And forever cherish the path of learning.

Ritual Leader: ____(name*), you come before us having completed a journey of learning and growth. How do you come to this circle?*

Graduating Student: *In perfect love and perfect*

trust, with the Fire of learning burning within.

Ritual Leader: *What do you offer your family?*

Graduating Student: (answer from the heart)

Ritual Leader: *What do you offer your Gods?*

Graduating Student: (answer from the heart)

Ritual Leader: *What do you offer yourself?*

Graduating Student: (answer from the heart)

Ritual Leader: *You have done well and now you shall prove yourself before family, self, and Gods.* (Hands the list of clues to the graduating student and sends them on their quest. While the child is on the quest, family members may sing, chant, or simply sit in silence holding the energy).

When the student returns from the quest, the object is returned to the ritual leader at the altar.

Graduating Student: *I have completed my quest and return successful. I ask that I may pass through the gateway of graduation with blessings on my journey beyond.*

Ritual Leader (inspects object): *You have done well ___(name). (Turns to those assembled.) Does anyone in this circle have concerns about the passage of* ___*(name) through the gateway of graduation?* (Waits for objections to be voiced. There should be none. All concerns should have been raised before this ritual began)

Ritual Leader to graduating student: *What would you ask of this circle on your next journey?*

Graduating Student: (answers from the heart within reason)

Ritual Leader to group: *Do we promise to do our best to give what has been asked?* (Waits for an answer.) *Do we vow to support and guide* ___(name) *in the journey to come?* (Waits for an answer.)

Ritual Leader: *I am honored to present you, before your friends, family, and Gods, this certificate of graduation. May you carry this in your heart and mind as a badge of honor and a base for future success.* (Hands certificate to child.)

Graduating Student: (offers thanks from the heart)

Ritual Leader releases the directions:

I give thanks for the blessings
of Earth, Air, Fire, and Water.
Thank You for Your guidance and protection.
Lend us Your energies, now and forever,
That our every action may honor You.

Ritual Leader releases the God and Goddess and any spirit guides who were invoked:

Dear Ones,
We honor Your presence
in this ritual and in our lives.
We are grateful for Your guidance
and assistance in this journey.
As this graduate moves forward with his/her life,
We ask Your blessings and protection for her/him.
Guard us all and guide our steps
That we may all live a full and honorable life
And forever cherish the path of learning.

Ritual Leader and Parent, or designated adult, raise arms together to form a gateway in the East. Graduate passes through and leaves circle first, followed by others. A celebratory dinner or outing should follow.

Becoming a Woman

There should be a fair amount of preparation for this rite. Not only should the daughter be instructed in ritual behavior and the role of menstruation in her life: physically, emotionally, mentally, and spiritually, but she should also have created a Moon pouch before the ritual. This is a bag that will hold objects of power, comfort, and connection to her Deities and guides that is specific to her Moontime. This ritual was written for a mother and daughter and can be expanded to include a Moon group or larger family.

Set up altar:

- Altar cloth: red, pink, deep green, or black
- Red and white candles and flowers
- Rose quartz and onyx
- Salt and warm Water
- Symbols of the Moon and the Goddess as Maiden and Mother
- Moon pouches
- Rose or jasmine essential oil

Smudge each other before entering the circle.

Mother casts the circle and consecrates it with smudge and Water.

Mother invokes the directions:

I give thanks for the blessings
of Earth, Air, Fire, and Water.
Guide us and guard us in this ritual.
Lend us Your energies, now and forever,
That our every action may honor You.

Mother invokes the God and Goddess:

Dear Ones,
Mother and Father of All,
We honor Your presence in our lives.
As my child becomes a woman,
I ask Your blessings and protection for her.
Guard her and guide her steps

*That she may become
a wise and honorable woman.*

The girl's mother states the purpose of this rite--to honor her daughter and celebrate her entrance into the Sisterhood of Women and the Mysteries of the Moon Lodge and to pass the torch of woman to the next generation.

The mother shares what she knows of Women's Mysteries. There is a brief discussion on strength and power of woman and the feminine energies. The importance of honesty, community, and support among the Sisterhood is reaffirmed. The daughter, as new woman, is asked if she is ready for her role as a strong, creative woman and if she accepts her power.

The daughter is then anointed with rose or jasmine oil. She is then blessed as a new member of the Sisterhood of Women.

The new woman then invoke her guides, guardians, Goddesses, calling upon one in particular to work through her this night and continue to work with her in the Mysteries as she comes into her power as woman. She offers her blessings to her family and vows to uphold the sacredness and integrity of both the Sisterhood and herself.

She will then act as ceremonial leader for the rest of the ritual.

Meditation[28]:

Feel roots growing down from your body deep into Mother Earth. Extend your self deep into Her center.

Feel Her energy flowing up into the soles of your feet. Feel this grounding, empowering, beautiful energy flowing up filling your entire body. Breathe this energy into your entire being for a moment.

Raise up your arms and send out branches into the center of Father Sky. Extend your self into His center. Feel this expansive, empowering energy flowing down throughout your entire body. Breathe this energy into your entire being for a moment.

Feel these two energies flowing through you at once. Feel them meet and merge together in your center. Feel their differences and how they balance each other. They seem to dance throughout you.

You overflow with this energy. Feel it completely surround your body. Send it out to your Mother. Send it beyond this circle out into the Earth and the multiverse. See this energy permeate all things and connect you to all of Life.

The new woman speaks of the interconnections of all life and how all our relations are sacred. She speaks from her heart of the role of women in this sacred plan and how she intends to fulfill her place in that sacred plan. She allows any messages to come through her (silently or aloud) from her special Goddess.

Mother and daughter embrace and kiss. They take some time to sit and talk: woman-to-woman. The daughter thanks her mother and vows to be a living example of female strength and to uphold the integrity of the family. The mother vows to be there for her daughter in this new journey and to help in any way she can, while recognizing that the daughter must find her own way and live her own life.

Daughter releases the directions:

I honor the blessings
of Earth, Air, Fire, and Water.
Thank You for Your guidance and protection
In this ritual and throughout our lives.
May we live our lives with integrity
That our every action may honor You.

Daughter releases the God and Goddess:

Dear Ones,
Mother and Father of All,
You have witnessed my transformation
from child to woman.
I honor Your presence in our lives.
I ask Your blessings and protection
on this new journey.
Guard me and guide my steps
That I may honor the God and Goddess within.

Both women are encouraged to write their feelings, thoughts, experiences in a personal Moon journal to be kept by the daughter.

Becoming A Man

There should be a fair amount of preparation for this rite as well. Not only should the young man be instructed in ritual behavior and on being a man in today's society, but he should also have created a personal power pouch before the ritual. This is a bag that will hold objects of power, comfort, and connection to his Deities and those guides will assist him in his new role as a man.

While menstruating women are automatically in a perfect space for visioning each month, men often need to work to attain that state of being. Visionquests and sweat lodges were designed to serve this purpose in many cultures. Certainly women can benefit greatly from such practices, but they can be particularly important for men. As a result, a period of physical exercise, a sweat lodge, or a small visionquest may be an ideal preparation for your young man before his Manhood Rite. This ritual was written for a father and son; can be expanded to include a men's group group or larger family.

Set up altar:

- Altar cloth: dark blue, green or brown
- Red and white candles
- Clear or smoky quartz and onyx
- Salt and warm Water
- Symbols of the Sun, the God, and your helping spirits
- Personal power pouch for the son

Smudge each other before entering the circle.

Father casts the circle and consecrates it with smudge and Water.

Father invokes the directions:

I give thanks for the blessings
of Earth, Air, Fire, and Water.
Guide us and guard us in this ritual.
Lend us Your energies, now and forever,
That our every action may honor You.

Father invokes the God and Goddess:

Great Ones,
Mother and Father of All,
We honor Your presence in our lives.
As my son becomes a man,
I ask Your blessings and protection for him.
Guard him and guide his steps
That he may become a wise and honorable man.

The father states the purpose of this rite--to honor his son and celebrate his entrance into the Brotherhood of Men and to pass the torch to the next generation.

The father shares his experience and understanding of life as a man in modern society. There is a brief discussion on strength, power, sensitivity, and the roles of warrior, guardian, healer, priest, and father. The importance of honesty, community, and support among the Brotherhood is reaffirmed. The son, as new man, is asked if he is ready for his role as a strong, creative man.

Once he accepts, the young man invokes his guides, guardians, Gods, calling upon one in particular to work through him this night and continue to work with him as he comes into his power as man. He offers blessings to his family and vows to uphold the sacredness and integrity of both the Brotherhood and himself.

He will then act as ceremonial leader for the remainder of the ritual.

Meditation[29]:

You are running through a forest. Faster and faster you run, feeling the strength and vitality of your body as you speed through the woods. You stop as you come to a clearing. In the center of the clearing is a huge man. He calls you to come to him. As you approach, he seems to shift his shape. You cannot tell whether he is human or animal.

Although he is a frightening sight, you continue to approach him. As you do, he grabs you by the shoulders and looks deep into your eyes. He probes your very soul as he asks you if you are ready to be a man. Answer him honestly and allow any emotion you may feel to flow forth.

As you stare into his eyes, you are pulled into his being. Within him, you experience tremendous strength. You know it is your responsibility to protect your loved ones. You look deeper and realize that it is also your responsibility to protect all beings and the Earth Herself.

Looking deeper, you hold a baby, then an injured deer with the greatest tenderness you have ever known. You realize that love and gentleness are strengths too.

Looking even deeper, you see the Goddess. She embraces you, and you realize that you and She are One. You realize that balance is necessary in all things.

Suddenly, you are standing before the huge man and he no longer frightens you. He kisses on the forehead and tells you how proud he is of you. Listen for any other messages he may have for you before returning to your body and the Circle.

The young man speaks of the interconnections of all life and how all our relations are sacred. He speaks from his heart of the role of men in this sacred plan and how he intends to fulfill his place in that sacred plan. He allows any messages to come through him (silently or aloud) from his special God. If he feels it is appropriate, he may share his experience of the meditation.

Father and son embrace. They take some time to sit and talk: man-to-man. The son thanks his father and vows to be a living example of male strength and to uphold the integrity of the family. The father vows to be there for his son in this new journey and to help in any way he can, while recognizing that the son must find his own way and live his own life.

Son releases the directions:

I honor the blessings
of Earth, Air, Fire, and Water.
Thank You for Your guidance and protection
In this ritual and throughout our lives.
May we live our lives with integrity
That our every action may honor You.

Son releases the God and Goddess:

Dear Ones,
Mother and Father of All,
You have witnessed my transformation
from child to man.
I honor Your presence in our lives.
I ask Your blessings and protection
on this new journey.
Guard me and guide my steps
That I may honor the God and Goddess within.

Both men are encouraged to write their feelings, thoughts, experiences in a personal journal to be kept by the son.

As you can see, magick and ritual can be integral elements in the homeschool experience. Magick is nothing more than the act of effecting change in one's life. Through the methods used to effect change on a magickal level, children add to their education and their self-reliance. They learn to think and act for themselves with a broader understanding of life and hopefully with a bit more wisdom. Just like academic education, magickal training places valuable and lifelong tools for success in our children's hands.

Chapter Ten
A Special Bond

One of the most beautiful aspects of home education is the unique bond that develops between parent and child and often between siblings. Our children are encouraged to think for themselves and develop a personal self-image within a deeply supportive and loving environment. They learn to think critically and solve their own problems.

Furthermore, while they have great respect for their parents, they recognize that we are human. This alone brings with it a unique bond. Rather than being demi-gods to our children until we become totally "uncool," we are people just like them that have chosen to devote our lives to providing them with the best we can possibly offer.

In many cases, we have given up the quest for big salaries or professional recognition in favor of a one-parent income in order to make home education work. I do not say this to make parents who make alternative choices feel bad at all. We all must choose what is best and possible for our families and us. That is to be respected no matter what the choice. However, homeschooled children have very obvious and daily evidence that we put them first.

As homeschooling parents, we get to know our children on a level that other parents rarely do. We see their struggles and successes. We are a part of each milestone and each challenge. We recognize and support their growth as thinking individuals and we respect them for who they are.

These are not merely our children. These are spiritual beings who have chosen to incarnate on this planet at this time for their own spiritual evolution. We have chosen this family together and, as parents, our role is to nurture and support them as they create their own lives.

Certainly as home educators, we are responsible for guiding them in learning what they will need to succeed in our society. But just as important, and many would say more important, is their spiritual and emotional well being. The responsibility for this is largely within parental control, particularly as home educators.

I would encourage you to listen to your children and trust them. Trust yourself and your spirit guides as well. Allow children their emotions and support the healthy development of self-knowledge. Speak to them with respect and honor what draws them, in education and in life. For in truth, education is life and vice versa.

Forget the desire to appear as though you know everything and are the perfect parent. Let your children know that you are aware of your mistakes and teach them, through your example, how and what you learn from those mistakes. Consider the fact that they are learning about how to be an adult through you. Are they better prepared by seeing an unreal yet seemingly perfect ideal of an adult and a parent? Or can they learn more and feel more confident in their own abilities by seeing us for what we are?

These beings are the future of our world and, in many cases, the future of paganism. While they will certainly be their own individuals with their own belief systems, we can do much in the way of increasing the level of tolerance, understanding, education, and enlightenment in the world through how we live our lives, treat our families, and educate our children.

While some children may choose belief systems that conflict with ours, we stand a good chance of developing bridges of understanding and common respect by honoring their choices. The majority of children raised in pagan homes are likely to continue to honor the Old Gods, refusing to blindly follow religions that insist on the often violent elimination of disbelievers. It is this type of respect for Life itself that will eventually bring healing to our planet.

Pagan homeschoolers tend to possess an internal motivation, maturity, and discipline that I rarely find in those subjected to compulsory school. Rather than simply trying to spit back the right facts and fit into someone else's mold or gain someone else's approval, these individuals do what is right for them. They are encouraged to think for themselves. That alone is probably the best gift we can offer them.

Like many neopagans, these children have a clear perspective on what is acceptable in today's society yet they decide for themselves what path to take. They also have developed an incredible ability to network, create success, and structure life in a way that works well for them. They don't shrug off responsibility. Instead they have learned to be highly responsible because it is the right thing to do and because it is respectful of themselves and others.

This is a respect bred of mutual understanding and trust. Children do not belong to us. They are not ours to train or bring up in any predetermined mold. We have accepted the responsibility and joy to nourish them as they embark upon a journey of spiritual and personal growth. Through the experience of home education, we are all nourished with love, respect, and honor.

Appendix A
Homeschool FAQ

This chapter contains responses to some of the Frequently Asked Questions faced by home educators and anyone that may be exploring this option. Keep in mind that your experience may vary depending on how you choose to home educate and the dynamics present in your particular family. These responses should be viewed as a place to start when determining what works best for your individual family.

How do you afford it?

Home education is as expensive as you make it. You can spend a great deal of money going on expensive field trips and buying all the newest toys and supplies along with pre-packaged curricula. Or you do it for practically nothing with some creativity. It is all up to you.

Even inexpensive field trips can add up if you need to pay entrance fees once or twice each week. You might consider saving these types of events for once a month or less frequently. Supplement with the equally educational field trips to the local grocery store, the bank, and the gas station. Take a field guide or paper and crayons to the woods, the beach, or an empty field.

Homeschoolers in my area have taken the art of finding free events to a new level. I am constantly amazed at the field trips we can attend each month for free. We have done everything from handle bats to tour a beekeeping and honey-producing farm – all for free!

Utilize the free resources in your area. A good way to begin is to volunteer for appropriate local organizations with your children. An exploration of public or university libraries and the Internet should provide a wealth of free and inexpensive resources, lesson plans, worksheets, and "virtual" field trips. I also highly recommend using educational television, such as PBS, Discovery Channel, Animal Planet, the History Channel, A & E, and even the Travel and Weather channels.

Network with other homeschoolers for group discounts and to talk to the organizations in your area about the possibility for free tours and home educator's discounts on materials. There is a listing in the Resources section for A to Z's Home's Cool web site. They have a page that lists many of the companies offering routine discounts to homeschoolers.

In our area, we ask at local video, art supply, office supply, and bookstores about discounts. I had no problem convincing the university library to give home educators a healthy discount on books. The opportunities are out there. Don't be shy! Go ahead and ask.

Do we have to give up one of our incomes to homeschool?

Definitely not! I am a full-time writer, part-time teacher, and part-time wildlife rehabilitator while I homeschool full time. Sometimes the scheduling can be tricky, but I do not feel I need to give up anything in order to do what is best for our son. I know several people that work mainstream 9am-5pm (or more) jobs while very successfully homeschooling.

In fact, there are even email lists specifically for working parents, including single parents who work and still homeschool. More companies today are more open to telecommuting, part-time work, and bringing children to work. Some companies even have daycare on site to assist working parents. It is true that a support system can be very important, particularly if you are a single parent, but it can be done. How you work this out will also depend on your schedule, how many children you are home educating, and what their ages are.

Is it Legal?

It is in North America. In other parts of the world, laws will depend on the country. I have a friend who visited family in Holland during the summer of 2000 where she interested her sister-in-law in home education. The sister-in-law called school system to inquire about home education. It took her a while to get someone with the authority to answer her questions and after she was finally told that it is not legal, she received an almost quizzical response that no one had ever asked about such a thing.

Even within North America, the laws vary. Therefore, it is important that you find out the specifics for your area. In Canada, each province has unique regulations. In the United States, each state has its own requirements and each school district may have additional specifics that are or are not allowed, such as participation in extracurricular activities or notification and record-keeping requirements.

You can find a great deal of information at local libraries and through homeschool groups in the area. However, to be completely sure, you should go directly to the school district or state department of education for specific requirements. Self-education is important in this endeavor because school officials may not fully understand the laws or may be hostile toward them. You need to go in with as much information as you can before asking them for help.

How do you get along with your children all day every day?

Allow me to answer this one with another question. How do you get along with your co-workers, your spouse, or other family members every day? You treat them with the same respect as you would hope to receive. You remind yourself, even when they are whining or yelling that they are spiritual beings, gifts from the Gods, on a path toward growth and so are you. You continue to do your best to see the lessons in each event, each encounter, and each argument. And you forgive yourself and them when someone loses control.

Communication and a consistent demonstration of unconditional love, coupled with the giving and expectation of respect and honor go much further than we realize, until we see them in action. Talk things through. Encourage journal writing and a safe expression of feelings. Don't carry grudges.

For metaphysical parents, we have additional resources at hand to handle this. We can have a child's astrological chart analyzed and compare it to others in the family. This can be extremely beneficial in determining learning and communication styles, as well as how our children feel and handle emotions. Through astrology, we can discover their needs in a variety of areas and get an idea of the lessons they incarnated to learn this time around.

Pagans can also call upon spirit guides and Deities for assistance. We can work with shamanic journeying, meditation, and ritual to clear our homes of negativity, get in touch with personal shadow aspects, and gain Otherworldly assistance in working through the tough times. We can pray together as a family and we can teach our children to gain assistance in all areas by interactions with spirit guides, Deities, and Nature spirits.

Am I qualified to teach my children?

You taught them to speak, to walk, to eat, to give up diapers, and a million other things until the day they were ready for preschool. You know them better than any teacher and you are eminently qualified to oversee their learning experiences. In truth, that is largely what we do in home education. We oversee and guide. We mentor and assist. We encourage and support.

Home education does not mean that you teach your children all they need to know all by yourself and from memory. There is a myriad of opportunities available and parents frequently learn right along with their children. Even when teaching subjects that you may have advanced degrees in, you may discover that you still learn as you teach and guide.

Families may make use of tutors, college courses, workshops, other homeschoolers, etc. Consider how much your child already knows about things you know nothing about. You did not teach them and yet they have found ways to learn, irrespective of what you do or do not know.

What about Socialization?[30]

Socialization seems to be the issue that most concerns non-homeschooling people and the one that elicits the greatest degree of amusement from homeschoolers. While it is true that some of us react defensively when faced with this question, most of us simply find it funny.

The fact is that most homeschooled children are so "socialized" that parents can get exhausted from all of it. Many of us participate in a wide variety of playgroups and homeschool field trips. Study groups are common. Less common in some areas are homeschool bands and sports teams. Home-educated children take classes in everything from painting to computers and from karate to acting. They take part in 4-H,

Scouts, and other large-scale organizations for children.

Our son Karl has two weekly playgroups plus science and chess clubs with other homeschooled children from a wide variety of economic and spiritual backgrounds. He plays soccer and attends karate lessons at least twice each week. We join others on field trips at least once each month. Karl has accompanied me on trips for my jobs and has observed my wildlife rehabilitation work since he was just two years old. In this way, he gains direct experience and it makes the learning come alive for him.

A growing number of homeschool families volunteer in their communities. Older children often get jobs, apprentice with adults, or enroll in college courses. Many pagan children participate in coven, grove, or community rituals. On my pagan parent's rituals email list for our community, there are thirty-six children and their parents and this list grows constantly. I organize children's rituals for most festivals and almost half of the children participating are also homeschoolers. Pagan gatherings are another wonderful forum for all pagan children to meet other pagans, including other children and community elders. We all learn from interaction with people of all ages and social backgrounds.

Socialization is frequently one of the reasons why parents choose to home educate. We object to the type of social learning that occurs in a traditional school setting. Our children are not limited to a same-age peer system under the absolute authority of one adult who teaches values we often disagree with. We prefer not to expose our children, particularly the young ones, to an often violent and non-supportive social structure. Since school violence is clearly on the rise, this has become a motivating factor for many new homeschoolers. We'll pass on that type of socialization.

Class size has become an issue of concern in many schools. When children are having difficulty learning or relating to other students, they are often placed in smaller classes or classes with a higher teacher-to-student ratio. The goal of these situations is a greater degree of one-on-one attention from the teacher and a reduction in unhealthy peer pressure. It is simply not logical to believe that the usual twenty to thirty students per classroom five days a week is more effective than individual attention received in a loving and supportive home with no time limits on learning.

When deciding on whether or not to home educate, availability of social interaction for our children is one of the main factors we consider. We want them to have beneficial and meaningful interaction with their peers just as much as they do. We want them to date, play sports, do plays, join bands, and whatever else they would have the opportunity to do in school. Parents name extracurricular socialization as one of the main reasons that some homeschooled children choose to return to public school. Therefore it is something that home educating families actively seek out for their children.

Socialization is also one of the biggest concerns for children who are going from public schools to home. The fear is that they will be sitting, poring over books, alone at the kitchen table. Fortunately, this is rarely the case. However, children coming out of public schools may be afraid that they will lose their friends and that is something that needs to be addressed with understanding and creativity.

As I wrote in the preface to this book, I have found a few situations where isolation did become a problem. This was usually due to parental choice and it is extremely uncommon. One might better ask why crime, addiction, teen pregnancy, and teen suicide are so common in our society. These issues were not so prevalent many years ago when our ancestors were frequently educated at home and socialized in much the same way that homeschoolers socialize today.

We must consider the effects of all our choices on our children, whether they relate to education or not. The reality of home education today is that children interact with a wide range of people. They are not isolated from social interaction. Quite the contrary, these children are encouraged to relate responsibly and maturely to everyone from infants to elders. From these experiences, homeschooled children learn respect, honor, and ability to communicate effectively that their traditionally schooled peers rarely do. This is socialization at its finest.

How much time should we spend each day on "school"?

That is also up to you. The best recommendation is to determine what works best for your family and each individual child. There is no cookie-cutter answer for homeschoolers. This is one reason why we do not turn our children over to the cookie-cutter mentality of most school systems.

Many parents have analyzed the amount their children actually spend in direct learning during their public school experience. Most have come up with anywhere from four to ten hours per week. Some school systems have programs for public school students who are "homebound" due to illness. In many areas, three to five hours of one-on-one instruction per week is considered to be equivalent for their purposes.

Children generally spend much more than ten hours per week at school. That amounts to just two hours a day for five days in a school year that has summers and other vacations off. Most homeschoolers educate year-round and consider that every experience is a learning opportunity. As a result, our children are learning all day every day. But they enjoy it because for them learning is a process of exploration rather than a forced march.

I like to think of home education as more of an age-appropriate college setting. For the most part, homeschoolers study what draws them and what they need to use in real life. You choose when and how best to learn. You can decide on the equivalent of a fifteen-credit semester or a packed twenty-one or more credit semester. As your children learn, they experiment and research what they find most intriguing. Best of all, you have plenty of time to play and learn through interactions with other people.

What about transcripts and diplomas?

Many people assume that children must be enrolled in some type of formal organization to qualify for diplomas and to obtain official transcripts. This is not the case and the need for such documents depends on what you choose to use them for. Documents can be provided by both accredited and unaccredited institutions.

Accreditation is often seen as being more legitimate or acceptable. This may be the case in some situations, but all it really means is that the institution paid an accrediting organization to review their practices. Those that meet the criteria of the organization are then accredited. Anything else is unaccredited.

It is generally assumed that to get into college, one must have proper documentation from an accredited school. It is true that some institutions, including military schools, do still require this type of documentation. However, many colleges, including several Ivy League schools, do not require a diploma at all and actively recruit from the ranks of homeschoolers. They do often require ACT or SAT testing.

Personally, it is important for me to keep records and I expect that I create my own documentation for Karl. But then I have three planets in Virgo in my house of work. I want to be sure we are covered just in case. I would also like Karl to have a record of the things we did for his own personal interest. This is not important at all for a great many home educators, particularly unschoolers.

The Distance Education and Training Council (DETC) accredits various distance learning programs and ensures that they meet certain standards. Most recommended programs are DETC accredited. Children of families who move frequently or are in foreign diplomatic or military service should consider using an accredited program.

Before making the choice to create your own documentation or pay a cover school to do it for you, do your own research and decide what is important to you. This is a wonderful project for children to be a part of. Determine whether or not diplomas from accredited schools are required for your child's goals. If your child has no concrete plan for adulthood yet, and many do not, decide what you believe to be important records to keep. Some people keep a daily log of activities while others are much more relaxed.

The GED (General Educational Development program) is always an option in place of a high school diploma. Some homeschoolers find that this option may not be the best one and tend to find other means to help with college acceptance. Some have found that the GED brings with it a type of social stigma associated with high school drop-outs. Some home educators report that the GED can create an unwanted focus on an application, requiring all other documentation to looked at more closely. It has even been suggested that those students applying to college or the military with a GED may be expected to show higher test scores and more extracurricular activities than other applicants. In any event, it is best to investigate this option fully before making any decision.

When creating personal homeschool transcripts and diplomas, it is important that you make them as complete and professional as possible without any embellishment. Be honest about your children's achievements and about their challenges. Some scholarship providers are more than willing to consider homeschooled children. However, several have had problems with incomplete and unrealistic transcripts. Also be sure to include extracurricular classes and activities.

One additional word on record keeping in home education: it is required by some states in order to homeschool. When in doubt, check home school requirements for your state and district.

Do colleges accept homeschooled applicants?

In a word, Absolutely! Across the United States, there are hundreds of colleges and other schools of higher education, such as vocational-technical institutes and universities, that not only accept but actively recruit home educated applicants. While many homeschoolers prefer to apprentice or work in place of or before college, if this is your child's goal, they need not worry at all about getting accepted to college after a home education.

What is Unschooling?

Exactly what form unschooling takes depends on the individual family. In general, it is largely unstructured, child-led learning that uses life experience to teach. The underlying belief is that children do not need to be taught to learn. The world itself is the ideal classroom. Children can and do learn very well if simply allowed to do so.

Unschoolers do not formally test their children.

They are not concerned about what children in public schools are studying. Learning is never forced. They follow the flow of interest and encourage children to get as in-depth as they desire with any particular subject. Full advantage is taken of life events that can be educational in any way. An area of interest for a child can teach a surprisingly wide range of "subjects." For example, an interest in karate can teach discipline, health, physical education, history, foreign language, mathematics, reading, social studies, and more.

What about moving from public school to home?

How this will be done needs to be seriously considered and discussed among family members. Children who are afraid of losing friends must be assured that this is neither the goal of home education nor is it likely to be a result. Time should be set aside for the child to be able to continue special friendships.

Most experts recommend a period of deschooling or detoxing after the child is removed from public school. This usually entails a time of rest and enjoyment without any focus on learning. This allows for the child to release the expectation of stress and rigidity involved in compulsory school. In this way, the child can more easily adjust to the more relaxed lifestyle of home education. Often this process results in the child's own natural curiosity to develop and, without any prodding, real learning begins.

Some homeschoolers suggest that you deschool until your child's creativity, curiosity, and interest lead you to switch gears. Others recommend deschooling one month for every year your child was in a public school. However, homeschooling is all about trusting ourselves and our children, not blindly following what the experts say we should. As long as you maintain your awareness, you will know when the time for deschooling is over.

In many cases, this is an ideal time to explore local homeschool groups or find online homeschool support for you and your children. This will give you and your children an idea of how many people and what types of groups are available. Your children may find friends immediately or you may need to try out a few groups before finding like-minded people. If there is a pagan community in your area, try to network with pagan homeschoolers. If not, consider posting flyers at metaphysical and health food stores for homeschoolers with similar interests.

Use this time as wisely as you can. Relaxation and enjoyment wonderful uses of time. This allows you and your child to really get to know each other again and deepen the trust between you. Another truly beneficial use of this time is to get clear on your own beliefs and expectations regarding learning and home education. Work towards your own self-knowledge and wisdom so that you and your children may create the supportive, healthy atmosphere you dreamed of.

What if we need to send our children back to public school?

We all hope that this will never be an issue, but we cannot pretend that the possibility does not exist.

Due to death in the family, loss of the primary job, or by the child's choice, this can become a very real possibility. As such, it is a good idea to keep up with state requirements.

It is a good possibility that your child will be tested for grade placement upon reentering the school system. Some schools will require documentation and transcripts. This enables the school staff to get an idea of what the new student has been learning and to determine what will be included on the official school transcript. It is best to be professional in your dealings with school officials and try to find those that are most helpful and understanding.

Unless you have reason to expect that this will become a real possibility for your children, it is not a reason to be overly concerned whether or not your learning experience parallels the learning stages in the public schools. Plenty of home educated children have gone back and forth to public school with virtually no problems. There is no reason to assume that in the remote possibility that this happens, your child will be any different.

How do I homeschool children with different learning styles or at different levels?

This can require some creativity and flexibility, depending on how many children you have and their ages. Even at very young ages, children do not require our constant focus. In fact, most learn best when left to their own devices with building blocks, books, etc. You may want to begin by setting up a flexible schedule to focus on each individual child for an hour or so periodically throughout the day. Set the others up with some play or study time while you work with the others.

Try to find some things your children can do together, like playing games or creating art. Field trips and hikes can be a great thing to do together. See if you can go with a group of children of various ages or at the ages of the children needing less of your attention so you can focus on the other child. Homeschool groups can be a tremendous help to families with children at different ages or with very different learning styles.

Unit studies may be quite helpful in this situation. In this way, children of different ages, levels, and learning styles can all study the same general topic together. However, they can all learn at their own paces and explore the topic in their own unique ways. A baseball unit study can manifest as an essay on history for one child, designing a baseball computer game for another child, crafting a personalized baseball uniform for another, and designing the ideal baseball stadium for yet another child.

You should also keep in mind that children learn from each other, even those with vastly different learning styles. Have older children or those that are more advanced in certain areas work with the other children, under your supervision at first. When they are old enough, discuss learning styles with them and have them try to learn from the styles of siblings. At the very least, they will learn to interact effectively with a wide range of people

How do I care for my baby while I homeschool?

The same way you do when everyone is home together in the evenings or on weekends, with a bit more flexibility. Take full advantage of the baby's naptime and any time when another adult may be home. Enlist the support of family and friends if possible for babysitting. Ask homeschool friends if they might take your child along on a field trip while you stay home with the baby.

Do I need special training to homeschool a Special Needs child?

Not at all. If you have parented a child with special needs to school age, chances are you know all the basics already. To broaden your understanding of the condition and any new techniques, it helps to continue to educate yourself in order to stay current. Explore the Internet and new books or try a subscription to relevant periodical.

How do I know they are learning? What about testing?

Some states require testing for homeschoolers. Before making any decisions, educate yourself on the requirements for your area. Many parents feel that testing is not necessary. We know when our children are learning and when they are not grasping certain concepts. Some believe that testing can be dangerous because of its potential to influence self-esteem and switch the focus of education from learning to getting good test scores. Other families feel that testing is valuable not only in gauging learning but also in preparing children for standardized college entrance or other exams.

If you opt not to test your children, then that is the end of it. If you do decide to test, then you need to decide how to test. Boxed curricula and textbooks offer prepared testing materials for each subject. Several Internet web sites offer printable test questions and online tests, some of which may be customized to fit your needs.

Standardized tests are designed to track average status at any given age for a large number of students. They only include certain basic subjects and should not be considered to be predictors of individual progress or intelligence. These tests can often be obtained though school systems and educational tutoring organizations. They may also be ordered though curriculum and testing companies.

Can my children participate in any of the programs available through public schools?

This will depend on the state and local district. Public school systems are not required to offer their programs to homeschoolers, even though most of us are still paying school taxes. Some schools, either by choice or legislation, will allow homeschoolers to participate in sports or band. Some do have a part-time program that makes certain courses and activities available to home-educated students. The best thing to do if you are interested in this option is to open friendly discussions with your local school district.

How do I find out about homeschooling in my state?

If you have a computer, this should be relatively easy. The National Home Education Network and the American Homeschool Association have legal information pertaining all fifty of the United States on their web sites. You can also check your state's legislative web site for any legislation regarding home education.

State and local school systems should have a department of alternative education or something similar. Both home education and charter schools will fall under this category. These departments often have literature on laws and resources that can be mailed to you. Smaller school systems may not have a separate department. If they cannot help you, go to your state's department of education.

Networking with homeschoolers in your area is an excellent way to find out what the regulations are and how to find out how to register. Libraries can be of great help in this search when you don't know anyone to point you in the right direction. Home Education Magazine is another wonderful resource that can also assist you in tracking down local information.

Resources

Diplomas and Distance Education

American School
2200 East 170th Street

Lansing, IL 60438
800-531-9268 (24 hours)
708-418-2800 (9AM to 3 PM)
http://www.americanschoolofcorr.com/

Citizen's High School
PO Box 1929
Orange Park, FL 32067-1929
http://www.citizenschool.com/general.htm

Clonlara School
1289 Jewett
Ann Arbor, MI 48104
734-769-4511
Fax: 734-769-9629
clonlara@wash.k12.mi.us
http://www.clonlara.org/index022.html

Goddess Moon Circles Academy
Box 129
Madras, OR 97741-0029
541-546-6108
gmcaenroll@goddessmooncirclesacademy.org
http://www.goddessmooncirclesacademy.org

Richard Milburn High School
14416 Jefferson Davis Hwy, Ste 8
Woodbridge, VA 22191
rmhsinfo@aol.com
http://www.rmhs.org/

Sacred Grove Academy (Alabama only)
C/o Church of the Spiral Tree
PO Box 186
Auburn, AL 36831-0186
Homeschool@sacredgroveacademy.org
http://www.sacredgroveacademy.org

Testing

Family Learning Organization
P.O. Box 7247, Spokane, WA 99207
800-405-8378 or 509-924-3760
homeschool@familylearning.org

Bayside School Services
PO Box 250
Kill Devil Hills, NC 27948
800-723-3057
testinghq@usa.net

Hewitt Homeschooling Resources
P.O. Box 9
Washougal, WA 98671-0009
360-835-8708 (for credit card orders)

Sycamore Tree
2179 Meyer Place
Costa Mesa, CA 92627
800-779-6750
sycamoretree@compuserve.com

Distance Education and Training Council
1601 18th Street, N.W.
Washington, D.C. 20009-2529
202-234-5100
Fax: 202-332-1386
detc@detc.org
http://www.detc.org/

The Mental Edge
http://www.learningshortcuts.com/

4Tests.com
http://www.4tests.com/

USA - State Information

American Homeschool Association
http://www.home-ed-magazine.com/AHA/HSIF/
aha_lws.rgs.html

Home Education Magazine
PO Box 1083
Tonasket WA, 98855-1083
800-236-3278
 Fax 509-486-2753
HEM-Info@home-ed-magazine.com

National Home Education Network – State Legal Information web site
http://www.nhen.org/leginfo/state_list.html

Pagan Scholarships

The Blessed Bee Scholarship
PO Box 2849
Norcross, GA 30091
770-840-9620
scholarship@theblessedbee.com
http://www.theblessedbee.com/scholarshipinfo.htm

Fly-by-Night Magical Resource Center
2275 North High Street
Columbus, OH 43201
614-299-7930
> Ohio State scholarship
> http://www.flybynightbookstore.com/
scholarship_local.php3
> National scholarship
> http://www.flybynightbookstore.com/
scholarship_national.php3

Appendix B
How to Speak Homeschool

This should give you an overview of most of the homeschooling terms you will come across in conversations or literature. This glossary will give you a head start on the lingo and prevent you from misunderstanding others or feeling lost. It will be particularly useful when reading the remainder of this book, especially the next chapter.

Autodidact: someone who is self-taught

Charter School: a public school receiving public funds and often sponsored by a community organization or board of education. The charter outlines the goals and procedures of the particular school. They are generally exempt from the laws governing other public schools in the district and may not charge tuition or discriminate in any way. These schools may offer programs, including home study, for home-educated students.

Classical Approach: Educational philosophy that approximates or parallels the traditional system used in most compulsory schools.

Compulsory School: see government school

Correspondence School: a distance-learning program that offers individual courses or full curricula that are administered by an instructor.

Cover School: also Umbrella School; an organization that offers home educators a variety of services in addition to the comfort of being part of a legal "school." They often provide record-keeping, student identification cards, curriculum counseling, transcripts, and diplomas. They may also offer networking assistance, newsletters, and even yearbooks.

Curriculum: a course of study; all that you will be learning, including materials, for a predetermined period of time, usually a semester or a year.

Boxed Curriculum: a pre-packaged curriculum that includes everything a public school would offer, including tests, worksheets, pre-set assignments, and textbooks. These generally parallel what a public school student would learn depending on their age range and grade.

Cyberschools: Internet-based correspondence courses.

Deschooling or Detoxing: a transitional period for a

child who has left public school. This is usually a time of no schooling or unschooling to allow a child to adjust before the family style of home education begins.

Eclectic Approach: Educational philosophy that involves using a variety of materials and methods.

Flexible Learning: usually offered by distance learning programs that function as umbrella schools with varying degrees of control. These allow parents control over curricula while the organization provides a certificate or diploma.

Government Schools: alternate term for public schools; also compulsory schools.

GWS: Growing Without Schooling Magazine.

HEM: Home Education Magazine with both online and print versions

Holt, John: a teacher, social critic, and author who gave up his idea of school reform in favor of unschooling for children. He is seen as an education pioneer and one of the founders of the modern home education movement.

Homeschool Group: a cooperative group of home educating families who meet on a regular basis for socialization, study, field trips, support, etc.

HSLDA: Home School Legal Defense Association. This is a controversial organization that offers some valuable information and resources but predominantly represents conservative Christian values.

Inclusive: including everyone regardless of religion, home education style, etc. This term is often used to describe groups or publications and to differentiate them from exclusive ones.

ISP: Independent Study Program; allows home learning of specific courses and curricula. They may function as cover schools and have varying degrees of control over coursework.

Learning Style: the way in which each individual learns best. There are several theories on this proposing a variety of learning styles and intelligences.

Manipulatives: hand-on objects, such as blocks and rods, to assist with learning.

R-4: filed by all private schools in California. This is one way of homeschooling in California. Some cover schools are R-4 schools as opposed to charter schools.

Scope and Sequence: detailed outline of the curriculum for any grade level
Socialization: social interaction; homeschoolers are often questioned about this in terms of interaction with playmates of the same age.

Support Group: see Homeschool Group

Traditional Approach: see Classical Approach

Umbrella School: see Cover School

Unit Study: an in-depth and integrated approach to learning in which a specific topic is the foundation for all educational activities for a period of time. This topic is the basis for math, science, history, art, etc. It offers a broader understanding of the topic, which can be anything from the Middle Ages, the solar system, the elements, the seasonal festivals, druids, and much more.

Unschooling: possibly the most misunderstood home education method. The term was coined by John Holt to denote education without public schools. This does not mean no education. It is child-led, usually unstructured education that utilizes real-life experiences and opportunities to support learning.

Appendix C
Good Books for Pagan Kids

This is a basic listing of books that are fun to read, thereby encouraging reading and language skills. They may be academically oriented, offer comparative spiritual studies, or speak to the values that are often taught in pagan homes. Sadly, a great many wonderful books are now out of print. Due to the difficulty in finding many of these books, I have kept this list to those books that are in print as of this writing.

Early Readers: approx. 1-6 years old

Amber K. (1998) *Pagan Kids' Activity Book.* Horned Owl Publishing.

Bang, Molly Garrett. (1997) *Common Ground.* Scholastic Trade Books

Berger, Barbara H.
    Animalia (1999) Tricycle Press

Grandfather Twilight (1984) Putnam
Gwinna (1990) Philomel Books
When the Sun Rose (1997) Paper Star.

Brett, Jan. (1992) *The First Dog*. Harcourt

Caduto, Michael et al.. (1999) *Keepers of the Earth*. Fulcrum

Cannon, Janell. (1993) *Stellaluna*. Harcourt

Cherry, Lynne.
   A River Ran Wild (1992) Voyager
   The Armadillo from Amarillo (1999) Voyager
   The Great Kapoc Tree. (2000) Voyager

Cross, Tom. (1998) *Fairy Garden*. Andrews McMeel

Jeffers, Susan. (1991) *Brother Eagle, Sister Sky*. Dial Books for Young Readers

Plourde, Lynn. through Simon & Schuster
   Wild Child (1999)
   Winter Waits (2000)

Rose, Deborah Lee. (2001) *The People Who Hugged the Trees*. Robert Rinehart Pub.

Zorn, Steven. (1989) *Start Exploring Bullfinch's Mythology*. Running Press.

Elementary Readers: approx. 6-10 years old

Bergsma, Jody.
>*Dragon* (1999) Illumination Arts
>*The Little Wizard* (2000) Illumination Arts

Bevan, Finn. (1999) *Beneath the Earth: the facts and the fables.* Children's Press.

Boritzer, Etan
>*What is Death?* (2000) Veronica Lane Books
>*What is God?* (1990) Firefly Books

D'Aulaires, Ingri and Edgar Parin. (1992) *Book of Greek Myths.* Picture Yearling

Gilchrist, Cherry and Amanda Hall. (19) *Sun-Day, Moon-Day: How the Week was Made.*

Hanken, Sandra. (1998) *Sky Castle.* Illumination Arts

Jackson, Ellen.
>Summer Solstice (2001) Millbrook Press
>*Winter Solstice* (1997) Millbrook Press

Loehr, Mallory - the magical elements series by Random House
>*Earth Magic, Fire Dreams, Water Wishes,* and *Wind Spell*

Ogden, David (1997) *Dreambirds.* Illumination Arts.

Rowling, J.K. the Harry Potter series through Scholastic Trade Books.

Older Readers: approx. 9 and up

Alexander, Lloyd.
> *The Black Cauldron* (1999) Yearling
> *The Book of Three* (1999) Yearling
> *The Castle of Llyr* (1999) Yearling
> *The Foundling* (1996) Puffin
> *The High King* (1999) Yearling
> *Taran Wanderer* (1969) Yearling

Burnett, Frances Hodgson. (1987) *The Secret Garden.* Harpercollins

Eager, Edward
> *Half Magic* (1999) Harcourt Brace
> *Knight's Castle* (1999) Harcourt Brace
> *Magic by the Lake* (1999) Harcourt Brace
> *Magic or Not?* (1999) Odyssey Classics
> *The Time Garden* (1999) Harcourt Brace
> *The Well-Wishers* (1999) Odyssey Classics

Hamilton, Virginia. (1995) *Her-Stories: African-American Folktales.* Scholastic

Green, Roger Lancelyn. (1996) *Tales of Ancient Egypt.* Puffin

Le Guin, Ursula. *The Wizard of Earthsea* trilogy through Bantam Spectra

McCaffrey, Anne. The Dragonriders of Pern series and the Crystal Singer series through Del Rey

McKillip, Patricia A. *The Riddlemaster of Hed* trilogy through Ace Books

Tolkien, J.R.R *The Hobbitt, The Silmarillion*, and The Lord of the Rings Trilogy through Mariner

Notes

[1] Ground out: meaning to eliminate these energies from the personal energy field, either consciously or automatically.

[2] Madden, *Pagan Parenting*, pp. 53

[3] see Appendix B: How to Speak Homeschool.

[4] Madden, *Pagan Parenting*, pp. 44

[5] Goddess Moon Circles Academy and Lytl Witch, see Resources at the end of this chapter.

[6] see Resources at the end of this chapter.

[7] See Appendix B: How to Speak Homeschool

[8] icons that denote facial expressions or emotions. For example, :) is a happy face.

[9] using the first letter of each word in a phrase as a type of short-hand. For example, LOL means laughing out loud.

[10] For example, *smile* or (just kidding)

[11] MIT News web site, http://web.mit.edu/newsoffice/nr/2001/ocw.html

[12] The onset of menstruation; one's first "period"

[13] Madden, *Mabon: Celebrating the Autumn Equinox*

[14] Rogers-Gallagher, *Astrology for the Light Side of the Brain*, pp. 25.

[15] Rogers-Gallagher, *Astrology for the Light Side of the Brain*, pp. 166.

[16] Madden, *Pagan Parenting,* pp. 150-151.

[17] Centered between your eyes and up a few inches into your forehead

[18] Madden, *Book of Shamanic Healing*

[19] Llewellyn 2001.

[20] Kidney beans are not recommended due to toxicity when raw

[21] usually vermiculite and potting soil mixture; found in garden stores

[22] The Celtic tree alphabet

[23] from J.K. Rowling's series of books, _2001 Warner Brothers.

[24] Grimassi, *Italian Witchcraft*, pp. 28.

[25] From Madden, *Mabon: Celebrating the Autumn Equinox*

[26] from Madden, *Mabon: Celebrating the Autumn Equinox*

[27] Adapted from Madden, *The Book of Shamanic Healing* (Creating a Physical Anchor exercise)

[28] Madden, *Pagan Parenting*, pp. 224-225.

[29] Madden, *Pagan Parenting*, pp. 227-228.

[30] Adapted from an article first published by Merry Begot Internet magazine (http://www.merrybegot.homestead.com/may01p1.html) in May 2001 as The "S" Word.

Index

Tool 15, 17, 21, 47, 94, 121, 128, 131, 134, 136, 149, 151, 157, 158, 160, 163, 170, 177, 202, 221-224, 227, 250
Toy 21, 64, 180, 194, 255
Tree 67, 79, 132, 135, 150, 173-175, 185, 193, 197, 198, 207-209, 211, 216, 217, 276, 285
Trip, see Field Trip
Trust 18, 21, 29, 31, 34, 35, 90, 96, 104, 132, 152, 158, 160, 181-183, 222, 239, 252, 254, 269

<u>**U**</u>
Unit 26, 69-75, 124, 128, 140, 156, 175, 187, 194, 196, 218, 227, 283
University 69, 77, 91, 92, 143, 256
Unschool 36, 57, 62, 66, 80, 112, 265, 267, 281, 283

<u>**V**</u>
Violence 10, 14-16, 18, 22, 28-30, 138, 262
Vocabulary 74, 155

<u>**W**</u>
Water 135, 136, 153, 157, 163-170, 180-182, 184, 188, 189, 191, 194, 199, 209, 234, 237, 238, 240, 242, 245, 246, 249, 286
Workbook 62, 64, 67
Worksheet 20, 59, 672, 65, 67, 76, 84, 108, 110, 256, 280

<u>**Y**</u>
Yoga 43

Spilled Candy Recommends:

If you have young teens you'd like to introduce gently to pagan spirituality, we recommend the following books:

The Temple of the Twelve
A Spiritual Fairytale
by Esmerelda Little Flame

ISBN: 1-892718-32-4
Published by Spilled Candy Publications, 2001
Available now!

Read a description at
http://www.spilledcandy.com/
TheTempleOfTheTwelve.htm

Pelzmantel
A Medieval Tale
by K.A. Laity

Published by Spilled Candy Publications, 2003
Available February 2003

Read a description at
http://www.spilledcandy.com/Pelzmantel.htm

Spilled Candy Recommends:

If you have like collections of tips, anecdotes, recipes, and ideas for pagans, we recommend the following books:

Gifts for the Goddess on a Hot Summer's Night by Lorna Tedder and Shannon Bailey

Published by Spilled Candy Publications, 2000
ISBN 1-892718-15-4
Available now!

Read a description at
http://www.spilledcandy.com/
SummerGoddessGifts.htm

Gifts for the Goddess on an Autumn Afternoon by Lorna Tedder and Aislinn Bailey

Published by Spilled Candy Publications, 2000
ISBN 1-892718-30-8
Available now!

Read a description at
http://www.spilledcandy.com/
AutumnGoddessGifts.htm

More in this series coming!

For free ebooks,
free articles and tips,
and novels and guides
for the metaphysically-minded,
please visit our web site at

http://www.spilledcandy.com

LaVergne, TN USA
15 September 2009
157783LV00003B/88/A